SWIMMING

SWIMMING

by Andy & Judy Wilson

The Oxford Illustrated Press

First published 1979 by the Oxford Illustrated Press Ltd

© Andy and Judy Wilson 1979

All rights reserved. No part of this publication may be reproduced, stored in a retrieval system, or transmitted, in any form or by any means, electronic, mechanical, photocopying, or otherwise, without the prior permission of Oxford Illustrated Press Ltd

Printed in the UK by B. H. Blackwell Ltd, Oxford, and bound by R. J. Acford Ltd, Chichester, for Oxford Illustrated Press Ltd, Shelley Close, Headington, Oxford

ISBN 0 902280 62 7

(Previous page *Photograph of USA swimmer Tim Shaw, winner of three world championship titles in 1975*).

Contents

Getting Started	9
Front Crawl	13
Backstroke	22
Breaststroke	31
Butterfly	39
Water Polo	48
Long Distance Swimming	52
Synchronized Swimming	55
Land Conditioning	59
Organization of Speed Swimming	61
A Summary of Swimming History	63
Appendix 1: Glossary	68
Appendix 2: Laws of Swimming	71
Appendix 3: Useful Addresses	74

Acknowledgements

Our thanks for their help in the preparation of this book go to:

British Long Distance Swimming Association
Arthur Burgess (photographer)
Glenn Craddock (swimmer)
Karl Craddock (swimmer)
Dudley Metropolitan Borough Council (by courtesy of whom the photographs of swimming drills appear)
Tony Duffy (photographer)
Dave Rogers (photographer)
Clive Rushton
Karen Tether (swimmer)
Tracy Tether (swimmer)

and to all the other people, swimmers, parents, coaches, and officials who have influenced, consciously or not, the writing of the book.

Foreword

I am delighted to be able to write this foreword since I have known the authors Andy and Judy Wilson for many years. Both of them achieved an exceptionally high standard of performance in competition at international level and they have stayed in the sport when all too often swimmers of their calibre drift out and are lost. They have an enormous bank of knowledge and experience, which they have called upon successfully in this book.

The purpose of the book is to bring to the notice of any young swimmers the way to follow up any natural ability they may have for competitive swimming. There is a great deal of swimming teaching going on in Britain and other countries, mainly at school level, and it is for these swimmers in particular that the book has been written. Apart from guiding and helping potential swimmers into the competitive side of the sport, the book will aid everyone who wants to improve his or her technique.

There will never be too many books on swimming as there are so many different ways of approaching the technical aspects of a stroke. The wide experience these two authors have on the subject (Judy worked as my assistant at Beckenham for a few years) is shown in the chapters on the strokes and this book will make a valuable contribution to swimming literature.

Competitive swimming opens up a whole new world to youngsters who are interested in a challenge and the self discipline involved. Andy and Judy Wilson's book will certainly help to get them started.

Alan Hime
President, British Swimming Coaches Association

Looking down on the pool used at the 1972 Olympic Games in Munich. Notice the eight lanes marked by the black lines on the pool floor and divided from each other by lane ropes, with the swimmers settled into a spearhead formation.

Getting Started

This book is about swimming and it has been written for swimmers. It is not written for parents, though mothers and fathers may enjoy reading it. And it has not been written for teachers and coaches, as most of what it contains will be fairly well known to them. Instead, it is about what swimmers do, or may do, to improve themselves.

Today almost every child can swim. Some can just struggle up the length, but they can swim nevertheless. Because almost everyone at school can swim there are many children who have experienced competitive swimming. Most of these have probably belonged to a club or training group at some time or another. Others, who perhaps just fitted into a club team or got on well with the other swimmers, have no doubt stayed in swimming and have done well. But the vast bulk of swimmers are those who either just don't make it or only just do make it. They are the swimmers who reach county age-group finals but don't get into the first three, the swimmers who make up relay teams, the swimmers good enough to swim for their school and enjoy it, but who don't make the local club team. It is for these people that this book has been written, in the hope that somewhere in its pages there will be

Eleven-year-old age-group swimmers starting in the Southern age-groups at Crystal Palace.

One swimmer who has found it necessary to change clubs is Liz Taylor. She justified her moves by winning the ASA 100 metres butterfly title (1976).

something that will help them go faster, or if they don't go faster then still enjoy some kind of swimming sport.

Swimming is not just racing, or speed swimming. It is a number of activities organized under a large umbrella. In England this umbrella is the Amateur Swimming Association, the ASA, and there are similar bodies in other countries. The ASA, and its counterparts, governs not only competitive speed swimming but diving, water polo and synchronized swimming, and also has an interest in long-distance swimming. All these activities are interlocked not only through the governing body but also through the people who take part, as no single branch of the sport is the preserve of a single group of people. For men, speed swimming and water polo, or water polo and long-distance swimming often go together. For women and girls speed swimming and synchronized swimming are often indulged in by the same swimmers, while some speed swimmers are also more than competent long-distance swimmers. Diving, as a gymnastic art practised in an aquatic setting, is the odd man out and so is not dealt with in this book.

Because of this continual overlapping, the book deals largely with the techniques of speed swimming and describes not just the strokes but the ways in which swimmers, practising alone or in a group, can improve their performance. It also seeks to introduce young swimmers, who have possibly never seen a water polo match, a synchronized swimmer in action, or a long-distance race in progress, to these other branches of swimming.

About Speed Swimming

Speed swimming, or competitive swimming as it is also known, is about getting from one end of the pool to the other as fast as possible. It is also the sport most widely indulged in by school children. Through television it can be seen at its highest level—in the Olympic Games or the world championships.

Because of various constraints, not the least of which is the sheer expense of proper facilities, swimmers in the younger age range, up to about 14 years, seldom get a chance to take part in any swimming activity other than speed swimming. But at that age there is so much to learn simply about the four standard strokes that this is, to many, a good thing. There is plenty of time later to branch out into the other water sports, and a sound basic ability in the four strokes and a good background of fitness will stand you in good stead for the others. Many swimmers never have to leave speed swimming as it provides such a wonderful outlet of activities, social as well as sporting.

All this is to jump ahead. The essential, the first object, in any swimmer's mind must be technique. It is all very well being able to dive in and belt out a short distance on one stroke, but a more rounded enjoyment is had by those people who can fit into a team for any event. There are, it is true, some who never get the hang of breaststroke, and there are some people who can swim a beautiful natural breaststroke who never quite grasp backstroke. Others imagine that to swim butterfly demands superhuman strength and endurance. But with only a little application and practice almost all young swimmers can learn all the strokes.

Although you may read this book and try out the drills and exercises described in it, the chances are that if you swim on your own you will first get fed up for want of company, and secondly never have the priceless advantage of tuition. So you have to find a club. There can be few towns with a pool that do not also have a club. Some clubs are high-powered affairs organized for the training of international swimmers, while others are very modest. But essentially their aims are similar—to help swimmers better themselves.

Once you have joined a club, and there are some parts of the country in which it seems that every child has at some time or another belonged to a swimming club, you will find yourself in a new world, and it may soon become, after your home and school, the centre of your whole life.

You will get three main advantages from a club. The first is that all clubs organize, or should organize, regular competitions against other clubs as well as between their own members. It is in races that you will discover how good a swimmer you are and how you are developing as a swimmer. The second is that clubs offer training facilities—the water and the coach. Thirdly, and perhaps the most important, is that the club will introduce you to a whole new circle of friends, many of whom will remain your friends for the rest of your life. Even if your stay at a club is a short one, you will find the experience a rewarding one.

As we have said, there are disadvantages in trying to train or practise alone. And even for older swimmers there is little immediate pleasure in trying to fit even the simplest and shortest workout into a pool occupied by other people who do not share your enthusiasm for swimming up and down. So to begin with at least, you will find the swimming club a better place to practise. For one thing the company of other swimmers makes swimming a much more enjoyable sensation. For another the swimming workout itself will have been planned by the club coach to fit into a sensible training scheme. Naturally, there are

The trust and confidence of swimmer in coach and of coach in swimmer is a crucial element in the careers of both. This relationship is present in all levels of swimming.

some people who can find a clear pool and can train there: they are the lucky ones. But for most swimmers the club or some independent training group is the only place for serious training.

A Word about Swimming Clubs

As you become more involved in the activities of a swimming club you will find that swimming becomes more important to you. You will probably want to get into the club team for matches, and if you are only in the relay squad you will want to make sure of an individual swim. Or there may be an important local event—a schools championship or a county age-group competition—you would like to do well in. Whatever the reason there is a good chance that at some point you will say to yourself 'I want to get better'. And at this point you have changed from being merely an interested bather to a competitive swimmer. There is nothing calculated to make life more enjoyable or more interesting than for you to have a definite ambition. Now we don't want to be accused of writing the end of the

Age-group swimmers training at the Rock Aquatics Coaching Centre in Rochdale.

book before it has started, but it may be that the club you join doesn't quite suit you. There are many reasons for this, but the reasons may be that the club, through no fault of its own, does not offer you quite what you want. For instance, you may find it does not promote synchronized swimming—and not many clubs do. Possibly it does not encourage swimmers to swim in county competitions, or perhaps you may feel that you haven't been selected for teams when you should have been. The best course in such circumstances is for you, or your parents, to have a quiet—a very quiet—word with the club's secretary, and to listen to what he has to say. It is a very unusual club that satisfies all its members all the time. And it is a very occasional swimmer who is happy all the time. Human beings just aren't like that. However, most swimmers stay with one club all through their swimming careers and often for long afterwards. Only very rarely is it necessary to change clubs. And then as a last resort.

Front Crawl

Although there is no stroke described in the rules of swimming as 'front crawl', it is the stroke invariably used in 'freestyle' events and on the freestyle leg of medley races. This is because front crawl is the fastest stroke so far developed. It first became popular among competitive swimmers in the first decade of this century, and although it was first used in only short-distance races it soon became the only stroke to stand a chance in freestyle races.

The rules for a freestyle race are simple. The swimmers simply have to cover the set distance without walking and to touch at the turns and finish with some part of the body—the feet or hands. Precisely how they swim is up to them.

The Stroke

Most people reading this book will have a good general idea of what the front crawl stroke looks like. The illustration of the stroke is an ideal one. It is doubtful if anyone swims quite like this, but it

Below: *Australia's Jenny Turrall, whose quick-stroking two-beat crawl won her Commonwealth Games and world championship gold medals.*

1. The six-beat crawl, in which there are six leg beats to each complete arm cycle. Here the right hand is entering the water as the left leg begins to kick.

2. The right hand feels for the water as the left arm is about two-thirds of the way through its pull—the catch-up feature of the crawl.

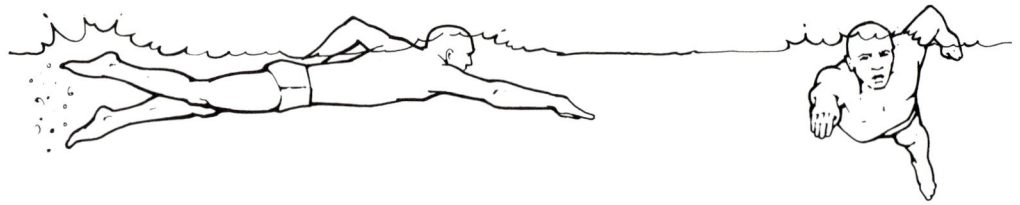

3. The left arm begins the recovery, bending at the elbow and swinging forward. The head is kept still and the right arm has pulled down.

4. Halfway through the right arm pull with the arm bent and the elbow kept up. The left arm has now come level with the shoulder.

does give a clear picture of the basics of the stroke.

The front crawl is swum with the body face down in the water lying fairly flat. The body rolls from side to side, onto the right side when the right arm is pulling and the left recovering, and onto the left side when the left arm is pulling and the right recovering. It is important that the body rolls for two reasons: it makes it easier for the breath to be taken and for the non-pulling arm to recover, and it allows more muscles to be used in the pull.

The head remains still throughout the stroke except when a breath is to be taken when it should be turned—not lifted—to the side. You can then breathe without interrupting the flow of the stroke.

The arm stroke is the most important feature of

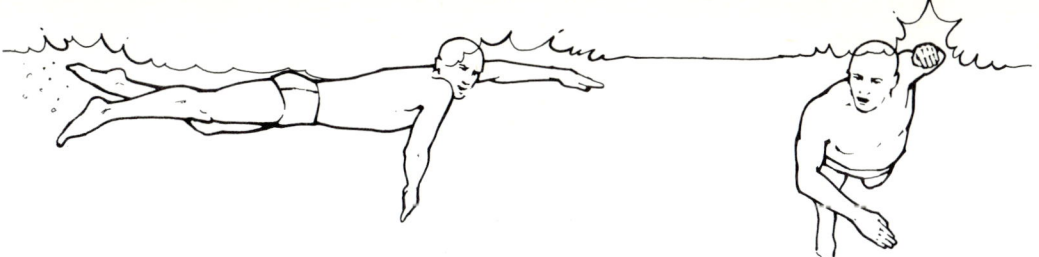

5. As the left arm enters the swimmer's head begins to turn to the right to take the breath and the right arm has just passed the half way point.

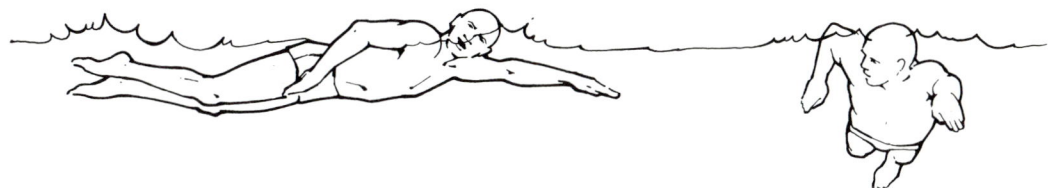

6. Just before inhaling, normally in a small hollow or trough caused by the swimmer's bow wave, the left hand is feeling for the catch.

7. Inhaling as the right arm makes the first half of the recovery. The head will be turned to the front as the right arm comes forward.

8. The inhaled breath complete, the head is now almost completely returned to the front as the right hand prepares to make its own entry.

front crawl, as most of the swimmer's speed comes from the arms. Some swimmers—very successful ones—rely almost totally on the arms for propulsion. The arms pull alternately, windmill fashion, though as we will see later they do not act entirely in opposition, as the arm recovering (coming forward over the water to start pulling) tends to catch up the arm actually pulling underwater.

The hand enters the water ahead of the shoulder with the arm almost fully extended, but not stretched, forward. The hand is then sunk into the water until, when it is about six inches down, pressure starts to be felt against the palm. This is the 'catch point'. From now on, to achieve forward movement, you will be trying to pull your body forward past your hand, not simply to pull your hand back past your body. Because your hand will tend to move the water, it is quite natural for it to move about during the pull. All swimmers do this, and the picture shows the path of the typical swimmer's hand when seen from below. From the catch point you should pull your hand back and down, trying to keep your elbow up and your hand ahead of your elbow, bending your arm gradually until it is almost at right angles as it passes under your shoulder. Then the hand is pushed back until it brushes the top of your leg. This completes the pulling phase of the arm stroke.

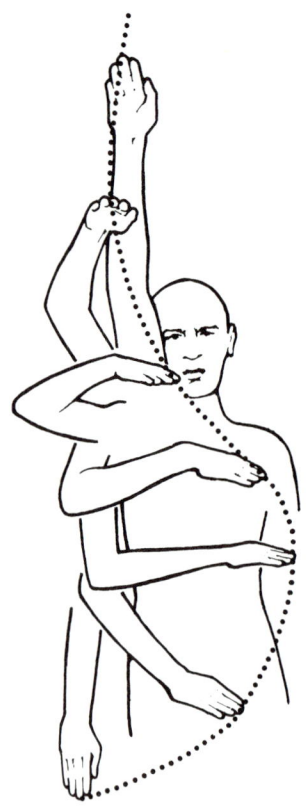

The front crawl pull seen from below. The hand enters the water ahead of the shoulder and pulls back, crossing the body during the roll, and exits close to the top of the thigh.

The hand is returned to the starting position of the pull above the water. As your hand reaches the back of the pull the elbow is lifted, the shoulder of that arm comes out of the water due to the roll onto the other arm (which has now started its own pull) and is swung forwards to recommence its own stroke. The arm is normally bent and then straightened during this part of the arm stroke, which is called the 'recovery'.

Some swimming teachers place great emphasis on the front crawl leg kick. Although the legs do not add much speed to the stroke it is important for almost all swimmers, except perhaps those quite unable to kick front crawl at all well, to practise the leg kick. It provides a sound foundation to the rest of the stroke, balancing the body naturally, and provides a rhythm for the tiring swimmer. The big muscles at the top of the leg need a lot of energy, and it is important to keep them in good condition.

The action of the leg kick is quite simple. The kick is an alternate vertical flutter kick. The legs appear to be straight, but bend slightly at the knees. With the natural whip of the ankles on the down beat a forward propulsive force is obtained. Once you have the idea of the kick it becomes quite natural and easy.

The breath in front crawl is made by turning the head to the side, the turning of the head taking the mouth clear of the water. It is important that the head is turned, and not lifted. If you find it easiest to breathe to the right, you will find your head will turn almost without conscious effort to the right as your right arm begins its recovery, and you will have completed the 'in' breath before your arm passes your face. As your right arm enters the water to pull so your head will have returned to the front. The 'out' part of the breath is then made while your face is in the water.

Most swimmers breathe on every right or left arm recovery, once to every two arm pulls. Some find it convenient to breathe every three strokes, so that they breathe to alternate sides. Others like to breathe to one side of the pool all the time, so they will breathe to the right on one length and to the left on another. All swimmers should be able to breathe easily to either side, especially in the longer races.

The natural timing or rhythm of front crawl is six leg kicks for each complete arm cycle (right and left arm strokes). Although most swimmers find they swim like this quite naturally, some find that two or four leg kicks provide a more comfortable pattern. Still others find their legs cross over during the stroke. These are acceptable variations on the general pattern, and if your stroke develops like this don't worry. Every Olympic champion has some individual quirk in his or her stroke!

Five Points to Remember

It is not important to copy someone else's stroke slavishly or to conform to some ideal type of stroke. But it is important to do the important things properly. So when you swim, think of these five points.

1. Feel the water. When your hand goes in feel for the pressure of the water on your fingers, your palms, and your forearms. Try to keep this pressure on your hand all through the pull.
2. Push out at the back. There isn't much propulsion to be gained from the push at the back, but if you do this 'follow through' properly, the rest of your stroke will benefit.
3. Keep your elbow up. During the recovery especially, lift your elbow high and let the rest of your arm relax. Keep your elbow up during the pull too.
4. Roll. Don't try to swim with your body flat in front crawl. Roll for two reasons: to make the recovery easier, and to apply more force on the pulling arm.
5. Catch up, don't windmill. All good freestylers have a catch up in their strokes, and you will

The marked body roll of Shane Gould, who not only held world records at every freestyle distance but won an Olympic individual medley title as well.

We can learn a lot from this shot of another Australian, Sonya Gray. The catchup is clear here, with both arms well underwater, and so are the bent arms and high elbows of the expert front crawl swimmer.

almost certainly have this naturally. If you don't, get your coach to put it right.

Front Crawl Training and Practices

Front crawl is the stroke swum most commonly in training by most swimmers, and a front crawl specialist competing in district or national events can expect to swim as much as 90 per cent of workouts with this stroke. Most coaches will try to vary their workouts to keep the training interesting, and younger swimmers may find the percentage dropping to 50 or 60. We describe here some of the more common front crawl training practices (or 'drills') which coaches use to improve their swimmers' front crawl techniques.

Kicking is one of the two most widely used drills in training, on all strokes, the other being pulling. In kicking, or legs only as it is sometimes called, the swimmer uses only his or her legs and holds the arms still. There are a number of variations on this simple idea.

1. The high kick, in which the legs kick out of the water at the top of the kick.
2. The deep kick, in which the feet do not break the surface. This is the more tiring of the two methods, and less like the kick used in the full stroke.
3. With the arms supported on a float or kicking board. This is the most widely used method of kicking. One, two, or three boards may be used to vary the body position and the exact nature of the kick. Kicking boards themselves vary in size, from some very small boards which hardly provide any support to large ones with hand grips.
4. Without a kicking board, but with the arms extended in front. More tiring than No. 3, this drill is difficult to do without cheating, though good kickers will find it no trouble.
5. With the hands by the side or clasped behind the back. This is an advanced drill in which the swimmer will rely entirely on the kick for propulsion and for getting the mouth clear of the water for breathing.

Right above *Kicking, the basic front crawl drill. The kicking board provides support for the arms and eases breathing.*

Right below *Kicking without a float is more difficult, especially if you keep your fingertips just on the surface!*

Below *Kicking on the side adds a new dimension to kicking without a float.*

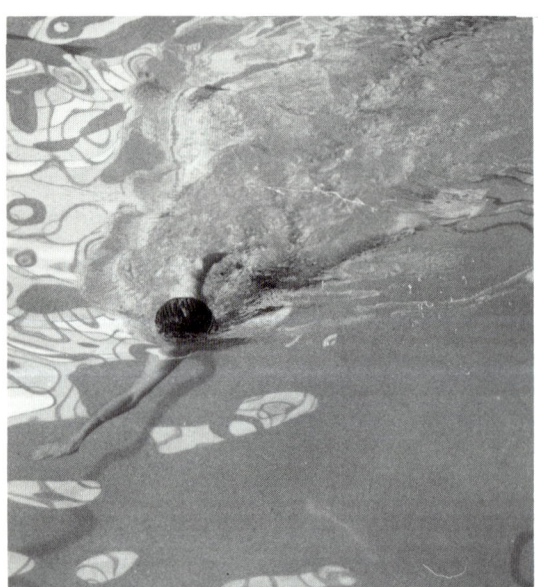

6. Pulling, or arms only, is the other common drill. Like kicking it can come in various forms, though most commonly it is done with the legs supported by a pull-buoy or float. Some swimmers use large rubber bands cut from car inner tubes to keep their legs still. Pulling and breath-holding—breathing every four or more arm pulls—are often used in combination.

7. The chicken wing. This is the first of a series of drills often done for fun but with a serious purpose. In this drill the legs kick normally but the arm stroke is restricted. The swimmer doubles his arms and tucks his thumbs into his armpits. Then he swims with the alternate arm pull, but in effect you will be swimming with your upper arm only.

8. Fisting. Like the chicken wing, fisting is not often used, but it is an interesting exercise. Simply swim quite normally, but instead of having your hands flat close them into a fist. You will, therefore, be swimming with your arms but

Top *Pulling, or arms only, with a small kicking board held between the thighs to add support—and to discourage kicking.*

Above *The catchup drill: the swimmer's left hand is about to enter, and as soon as the hands touch he will commence to pull with his right arm.*

not your hands, but you can get up some speed over a short distance. One word of warning: don't do this in a public session. If you hit someone you'll be in trouble.

9. Single arm, or the scooter. This is just the full stroke but swum with one arm only, the arm not being used stretched out in front. Breathe to the side of the pulling arm and concentrate on the catch, pull and push off the pulling arm.

10. Catchup. This can be thought of as the full stroke swum with one arm at a time or as the scooter swum using alternate arms. Starting with the legs kicking, pull one arm (keeping the other arm out in front) right through its movement until it gets back to the front. Pause, and then pull the other arm.

11. Stroke counting. Most swimmers have little trouble keeping count of their strokes and the number of lengths they have swum. A regular and consistent stroke count per length is a sign that you are swimming at a constant rate on a long swim. On single-length swims it is a useful exercise to try to reduce your stroke count without distorting your stroke.

12. Breathing patterns and breath-holding. As we have already said, front crawl swimmers should be able to breathe comfortably to both sides. Two practices help develop this ability. The first is to breathe to one side of the pool all the time. If you are in a race and placed in an end lane against the side of the pool you will not have the disadvantage of swimming blind on every other length. If you have a particularly dangerous rival, you will be able to watch him or her throughout the race. The second practice is to breathe on every third arm pull, so that you in fact breathe to both sides. Here again, you will be able to watch all your opponents in a race.

Breath-holding is a valuable training practice, as by forcing your body to work on less air you will make your lungs and blood circulation more efficient. In short races too, when it does not matter if you get out of breath temporarily and can make up for lack of air at the end of the race, breath-holding should be practised. In races of over 100 yards, however, regular breathing habits should be followed, and breath-holding loses its value. This exercise is one which should be done only at the request of an experienced coach and it is included here only for the sake of completeness. Don't try extended breath holding on your own.

The Start

The start of a race is always important, and it can of course be vital in very short sprint races of less than 50 metres. Almost all swimmers now use the grab start which was popularized by Mark Spitz in 1972 and enables them to enter the water quickly. The two vital aspects of this start are that you should pull yourself downwards to overbalance quickly before driving off the starting-block, and that the drive of your legs should be as powerful as possible. Once you get into the water, do not stay submerged for longer than necessary and begin your arm stroke smoothly as soon as possible. You should aim to transfer the speed from your dive into your swimming speed.

The explosion of the start as eight swimmers leave the blocks in the 200 metres freestyle final at the 1978 Commonwealth Games in Edmonton, Canada. Less than two minutes later the swimmer in lane 4 (fourth away from camera), Ron McKeon of Australia, won the gold medal.

Turns

If you have any ambitions at all in swimming any stroke it is vital that you learn to turn quickly and effectively. The fastest turn for the front crawl swimmer is the front somersault or 'tumble' turn. The best way to learn the turn is to do it in training whenever your swim is more than one length. The tumble turn breaks down into a front somersault in the tuck position (with the knees drawn up to the chest) accompanied by a half twist during the somersault and the push off to put you on your front as you come to the surface after the turn.

The secrets of successful turning are few. First, go into the somersault as fast as you can, speeding up into the wall during longer, slower swims. Secondly, make your tuck as tight as possible so that you can somersault quicker. Thirdly, make your push-off as strong as possible. You will be amazed how many swimmers spoil a good turn with a lethargic push from the wall. Fourthly, stretch out arms get into your stroke as soon as possible.

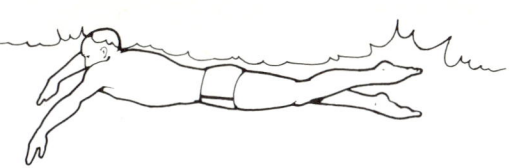

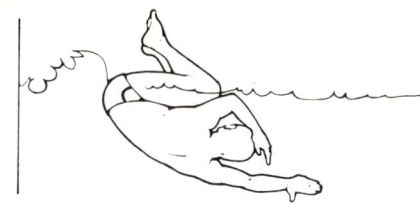

1. The swimmer approaches the turn, in this case making a double arm pull...

3. ... somersault but as the swimmer goes over he twists so that he is on his...

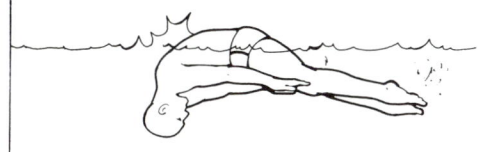

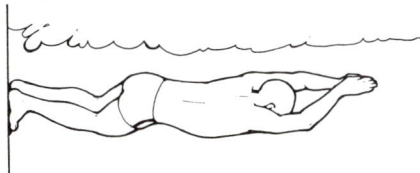

2. ... to give impetus to the somersault. This begins as a straight front...

4. ... side and ready to push off as his feet hit the wall.

The legendary Mark Spitz about to go into a tumble turn. His left arm will remain by his side while his right will give him the final thrust to make his somersault as fast as possible.

Backstroke

Just as in a freestyle race a swimmer can use any stroke he or she wishes, in a backstroke race any style or combination of styles of swimming may be used so long as the swimmer remains on the back. But while in freestyle events of any significance you will see only front crawl being swum, so in backstroke races only the back crawl stroke will be used.

The rules governing backstroke swimming are very simple. From a start made in the water a swimmer must cover the set distance while swimming on his back. He is permitted to go off his back momentarily at the turn but for all practical purposes, and certainly until you have mastered the flip turn, you should remain on your back the whole time.

The Stroke

Back crawl—or backstroke as it is most convenient to call it today—is swum on the back with the body flat along the surface; the arms rotate windmill fashion, pulling below the water and recovering above it; the legs perform an alternating flutter kick. So far it sounds very similar to front crawl adapted for swimming on the back, but in backstroke technique is important, especially the kick, whereas in the

Ambitious backstrokers could do worse than copy the relaxed head position of Mark Tonelli.

front crawl you can get away with many lapses from 'correct' style.

The best backstroke is swum with the body lying comfortably on the surface of the water with the shoulders slightly higher than the hips which lie below the surface to enable the leg kick to be made effectively. The high position of the shoulders enables the arms to recover more easily. Don't overdo this sloping position: your hips should be only slightly below the surface and your shoulders only slightly above it. If your hips sink too deeply you will 'sit' in the water, create an enormous amount of resistance, and swim slowly.

The head position varies from swimmer to swimmer, but in general it is held comfortably so that the ears are just above or just under the water. Most backstrokers keep their head in a position where the water level is somewhere between the crown of the head and the back of the neck, so that their ears are just in the water. The most important thing about the head is that it does not move: while the rest of the body is in motion, the head remains steady.

We must now look at how the swimmer actually propels himself. An efficient leg kick is essential in backstroke, and very few swimmers progress far without one. As in the front crawl the legs have a balancing and steering role, but in backstroke the legs kick affects the speed of the arm stroke as well as being propulsive in themselves to a far greater extent than in the front crawl.

The alternate vertical flutter kick of the backstroker has only a passing resemblance to the front crawl. The kick is deeper, between 12 and 18 inches, and although the feet should cause a slight splash they should not come out of the water. The legs should be relaxed so that the knees can bend slightly on the 'up' kick, and the feet pointed and slightly flexed rather than completely relaxed. There is no crossover or irregularity in backstroke kicking. Remember that a poor kick in backstroke cannot be compensated for by strong arms.

In backstroke the natural six-beat timing is universal among good class swimmers, there being six leg beats (three left and three right) to every one complete arm cycle (right and left arms). Only very occasionally will you see any variation from this rhythm. And if you want to accelerate and move your arms faster, you should first of all increase your rate of kicking. The arms will then follow.

The backstroke arm action is often described as a 'windmill'. The arms do in fact keep roughly opposite stations, and there is much less catchup than there is in the front crawl.

Another copybook stroke, the head still and relaxed, the arm coming over the water (recovering) vertically and about to enter little finger first.

Let us consider the right arm. The arm has recovered through the air and now enters the water straight but relaxed on a line in front of the shoulder. The hand should enter little finger first, though it is not wrong to enter with the back of the hand first and then immediately to rotate the hand so that the little finger is leading. The swimmer now tries to 'fix' the hand in the water. From the initial entry position the hand travels out and down, and as the elbow bends the arm starts to pull backwards, all at the same time. At first the hand will travel faster than the elbow, and you should try to emphasize this.

The arm is not kept straight during the pull. From the initial straight entry position it bends during the first 'pulling' half of the underwater phase, and then, having been bent at right angles, or nearly, at the hips the arm is straightened to complete the stroke.

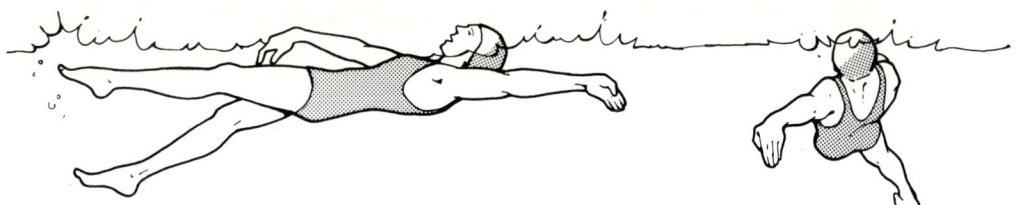

1. Just after the swimmer's left hand has entered and is beginning its pull, the right hand is about to leave the water and begin the recovery.

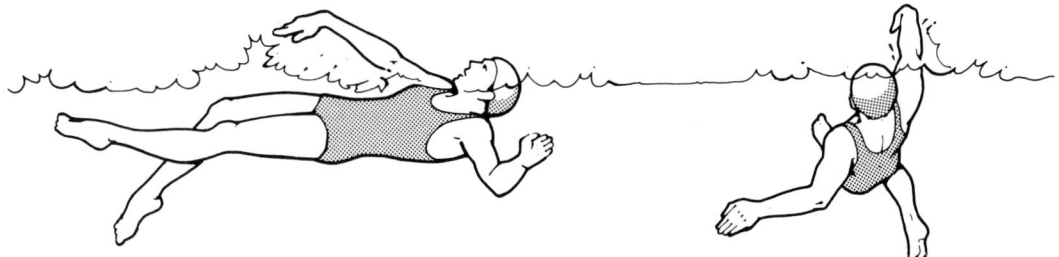

2. The pulling arm is nearly at the shoulder with the elbow bent. The hand of the recovering arm is quite relaxed.

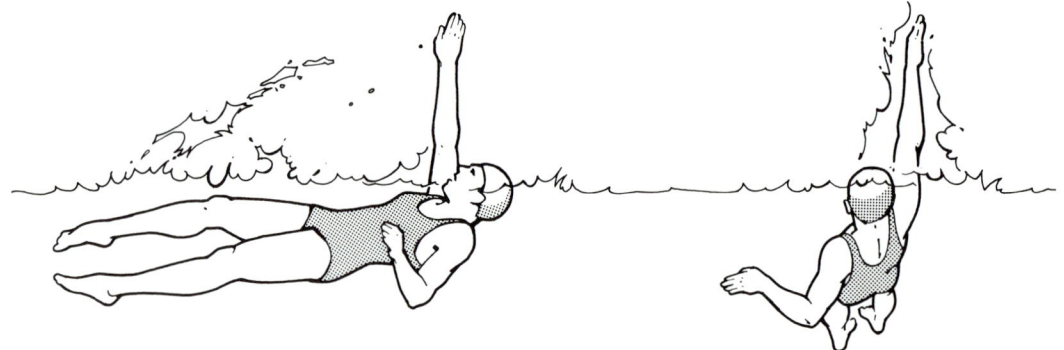

3. The pulling hand is now near the surface with the left arm well bent. The right arm recovers directly above the shoulder.

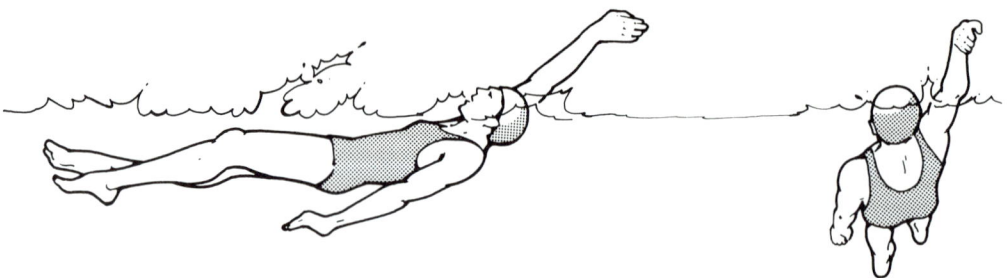

4. The left hand has now completed its pull with a final push down by the thigh as the right arm is about to enter.

5. The moment of entry with the right arm stretched ahead of the shoulder, left arm beginning to recover. The head has not moved noticeably throughout the stroke.

6. The cycle complete. The feet have not broken the surface nor the legs bent noticeably throughout the stroke. Note the 'whip' of the upward part of the kick.

The end of the arm pull is also important. You should try to finish off the under water part of the stroke with a strong push backwards and downwards so that your hand brushes past your thigh. Between the original entry and the finish of the pull it will be natural for your hand to follow the rough path of the letter 'S' when seen from the side, from which the term 'S-pull' for the backstroke pull comes. From the entry the hand goes down, along and then up near the surface when it is level with the hips, and down at the very end of the pull.

The roll of the body is not so apparent in backstroke as it is in front crawl. But despite appearances the roll is still there. The head, as we have said, should remain still throughout the stroke. The rest of the body—the shoulders, chest and hips—rolls to the right as the right arm enters, and stays inclined to the right as that arm completes its pull. The same, of course, applies when the left arm pulls. This roll has two advantages for the backstroker: more muscles can be applied during the pulling action; and the arm coming forward above the water can free itself from the water more easily and so reduce resistance. At the end of the pull, when the (say) right hand is pressing back and down the left arm is entering and as the body is then rolling to the left, the right hand is very close to the surface ready to be lifted out to begin the recovery. You might well re-read this sentence to make sure you understand how the roll of the body affects both the arm entry and the recovery.

The recovery in backstroke is very simple. From the back end of the pull the arm should be kept straight and then lifted upwards and swung forwards directly above the head.

The mouth is clear of the water all the time in backstroke so it is easy to forget about the breathing. Merely try to breathe regularly every right or left arm stroke. There is no advantage in backstroke in holding your breath for long periods nor in trying to breathe on every single stroke.

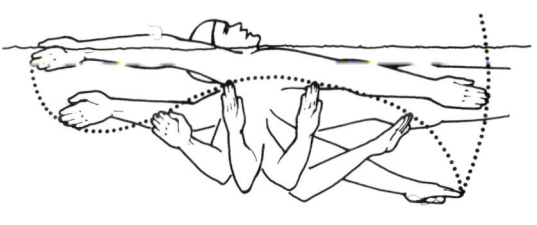

The profile of the backstroke pull resembles the letter 'S'.

Although the recovering arm should be straight, the arm pulling underwater must be bent to produce a strong backward push and to reduce the sideways movement seen here.

Five Points for Backstrokers

1. Keep your head still. Your head is your rudder, and if you move it around you will not be able to retain the smooth stroke necessary for successful backstroke.
2. The hand entry is made with the arms straight above the shoulder. Start the pull as far in front as possible.
3. Roll your body onto the pulling arm and get the shoulder of the recovering arm clear of the water.
4. Don't spill water from your hands as you pull: keep your hands facing backwards and your wrists firm.
5. Maintain a steady kicking rhythm, and if you want to accelerate, speed up your leg kick first.

Backstroke Training and Practices

If you are a specialist backstroker you will probably swim less backstroke in training than a freestyler will swim front crawl. You will certainly need to do plenty of kicking, for as we have already said the basis of this stroke is the drive from the legs. You will probably be asked to do longer slow swims on backstroke and some short sets of sprints, but you will not (or should not) be called upon to do the longer sets of repeats on backstroke. There is a great deal of what is called 'transfer' from front crawl and butterfly to backstroke, and your backstroke will improve from your training on those other strokes.

Kicking is the most important drill on backstroke, and fortunately there are many variations on it which help keep training interesting. All coaches and swimmers have their favourites, but here we describe just some of the many kicking practices.

1. With the hands by the side. This is the most natural way of kicking backstroke. Vary the stress by sculling—thus making it easier—or by holding your hands on your stomach—making it a little harder. Maintain the body position of the full stroke—head comfortable and still, hips just below the surface.
2. Alternate arm leading. You can protect yourself from other swimmers with the leading hand and practice turning on either hand, always turning on the extended arm. This drill can be varied by performing it on the side, which uses different groups of leg muscles.
3. Both arms extended above the head. Both arms should be stretched out flat on the water above the head. This gets the hips up, the body streamlined.
4. Other kicking methods. The three drills above are the most common, but there are others which it is useful to do once in a while. In one the hands are clasped behind the head, which means you have to kick harder to progress forward. There is also a series of drills in which the arms are held out of the water to make the swimmer kick harder to maintain his position: first, only the hands are held out, with the elbows tucked into the side; then, one arm can be held out of the water; further, try it with both arms completely out of the water—if you can kick for any distance like that you can kick pretty well!
5. Single arm swimming. We've already described single arm swimming in front crawl. In backstroke you can do it in two ways: with the resting arm by your side or extended. If you do it with the resting arm extended, remember to touch the resting hand with the swimming hand when the entry is made.
6. Catchup. Not as useful in backstroke as in front crawl, as it inhibits the roll, but like single arm it can be done in two ways, with the catchup taking place above the head (a useful way of getting nicely stretched out) or with the catchup at the end of the pull. Although you won't get the extension with this latter variation you will be able to practise the roll.
7. Double arm swimming. This is a marvellous drill if done well but next to useless if done

The initial backstroke drill—kicking with the hands by the side.

Another stage still—kicking with both arms above the head. This drill calls for a strong kick and complete control of the body, head and breathing.

Going one stage further—kicking with one arm extended, the other by the side.

A different kind of stress is added by holding the hands out of the water.

carelessly. Start with a strong leg kick with the arms above the head. Then pull with both arms together, remembering to feel for the catch early on, bending the arm half way through the pull, and ending the pull with a strong push back and down. Recover with the arms vertical and relaxed, entering the water with the backs of the hands together. Avoid at all costs entering with the arms bent or apart, and maintain your body position with a strong kick.

The Start

This is the only stroke in which the start is made in the water, and for this reason backstroke is the lead-off stroke in medley relays. Most pools equipped for racing have starting-blocks fitted with special backstroke start grips, and you should practise using them as much as possible.

The backstroke start is made as shown. At the command 'take your marks' pull your feet up until your toes are just below the surface and at the same time pulling your body up ready to spring back. When the starting signal is given release your hands, throw your head back, and dive backwards away from the wall. Don't fling your arms upwards, but throw them sideways out back level with the water so that they meet in front of your head. You should be able to travel for a short distance along and over the water, and then glide under the water for a short distance. After a second or two begin your leg kick and then almost at once the arm stroke, one arm at a time as in the full stroke. A good backstroke start can almost win you a race over a very short distance, and is very useful in any length race.

After the command 'take your marks' these swimmers have drawn themselves up on the starting grips, feet just below the surface and await the starting signal.

An ideal start by double 1972 Olympic champion Melissa Belote of the USA. She is travelling straight back above the surface, not going unnecessarily and wastefully high.

Finding the wall is every backstroker's problem. Look sideways and slightly forward for familiar landmarks without going off your back.

Nancy Garapick was a world record holder for 200 metres backstroke at the age of 13 in 1975, and subsequently enlarged her repertoire to include freestyle and medley events.

Turns

In backstroke, more than in any other stroke, it is important to be able to turn correctly. Mistakes are common in this stroke, and there are more disqualifications for infractions of the rules caused by lack of practice than by any intention to cheat.

Finding the wall is the young backstroker's biggest problem. By looking sideways at the pool wall you will soon be able to tell exactly where you are, and in major competitions you will usually find special backstroke turning flags strung across the pool about 5 metres from the end. After a time these flags will be the only check mark you will need.

Backstroke turns are best swum at speed, but at first it is best to practise them while kicking in to the wall. Kick in with one arm (let's say the right arm) extended above your head and pointing at the wall, and the other (left) arm at your side. About a yard from the wall sink your right arm so that your right palm will hit the wall about a foot below the surface and in front of your left shoulder. As your right hand touches the wall, the fingers pointing towards the floor of the pool, allow your arm to bend, drop your head back, and lift your knees up. Then, push hard with your right hand so that your head goes round to the left and your knees and feet whip round above the water towards your right hand, slapping onto the wall ready to push off. Meanwhile your left arm will unconsciously be balancing you and getting ready for the push off.

The push off is best made under water. Make sure you have both hands outstretched ready to get into the stroke as smoothly and as quickly as possible.

This version of the turn is known as the 'whip' turn and is extremely safe if you have practised it properly. The essential thing is to turn quickly and to keep within the rules. And to keep it legal you must not begin the turn until your hand has touched the wall and you must push off flat on your back.

The backstroke turn:
1. Below *The swimmer's right hand has touched the wall, about a foot down, and her body has already moved slightly to the left prior to her pushing her head hard away from the wall and* 2. Right *bringing her feet round onto the wall through the air.* 3. Below right *A strong push from the wall and into the stroke.*

Breaststroke

Although we have no accurate records of early swimmers, we can be fairly sure that the breaststroke was the stroke most commonly used in competition in the nineteenth century before the advent of the side and crawl strokes, and it was using this stroke that Captain Webb swam across the English Channel in 1875. The breaststroke we see today is something of a fossil, in that it has been preserved three times by changes in the rules of swimming. With the arrival of freestyle, breaststroke was recognized as a separate technique for competitions; after the advent of butterfly breaststroke, the two strokes were made separate; and when breaststrokers started to swim under water they were brought back onto the surface.

The rules define fairly clearly what breaststroke is, but there is still room for individual variation. The stroke is swum on the breast with the shoulders level and the arms and legs under the surface. The arms must pull back and be pushed forward (the recovery) under the water simultaneously; the legs too move together, being drawn up with the knees bent and kicking backwards with the feet turned outwards. Some part of the head must remain clear of the water at all times after the start and turn.

The Stroke

As the rules say, breaststroke is swum with simultaneous movements of the arms and legs. It is also useful to think of these movements being symmetrical, so that the actions of your right arm and leg are copied exactly as if in a mirror by your left arm and leg. You won't attain perfect symmetry, as nobody's body is perfectly symmetrical, but it should still be your intention.

Breaststroke swimming has been a feature of competitive swimming for over a century.

Above *Robin Corsiglia carried the Canadian maple leaf to victory in the 100 metres breaststroke at the 1978 Commonwealth Games.* Below *Karla Linke, ex-world record holder, is just one of the many stars brought to light by the East German training system.*

The body position in breaststroke should be as flat as possible. When the breath is taken the shoulders will be lifted somewhat but in general the shoulder position will vary from just beneath the surface to some distance above it. The hips should be well up to the surface but never, never, breaking it. The feet, too, should always be within 12 inches of the surface.

Some teachers tend to underestimate the propulsion to be gained from the arm stroke. Although it is true that the arms contribute less to the speed of the breaststroke than they do to front crawl and backstroke most breaststrokers gain a considerable amount of propulsion from their arm pulls, as much as a half with some stronger boys. The emphasis to be placed on the arm pull by any swimmer will be a matter for individual consideration, but in general the balance of propulsion from the arms and legs is roughly 40:60. Think of it in this way and you won't go far wrong.

The arm pull starts from a position in which the arms are held in front of the shoulders with the hands touching, palms down. You should stretch out as far in front as you can at this point, and the hands should be between 4 and 6 inches under the surface. The first stages of the pull are then similar to the front crawl. Feel for the water with your fingers first and then start to move your forearms before your upper arms. The pull is then semi-circular, with the hands pressing back. As in the front crawl, you should think of keeping your elbows up. The arms first pull outwards and downwards, and once they have pulled back to an angle of about 45 degrees you should bend your elbows and spin your hands in towards your chest so that they meet just beneath your breastbone, still keeping the palms facing downwards. At this point the breath is taken. Then, without a break in the continuous arm movement the hands shoot forward to the starting position again. It is worth always making sure that when you stretch forward you do in fact completely extend your arms so that the backs of your arms (the triceps muscles) feel tight, and although when you are racing your arms will be continually on the move you should, just for an instant, be completely stretched out. Apart from this instantaneous pause there is no glide at all in the racing breaststroke.

Above *Margaret Kelly, the latest in a British tradition of world class breaststroke swimmers, won a bronze medal in the 1978 world championships in Berlin.* Below *David Wilkie, winner of three world, two European, and one Olympic title in breaststroke and medley.*

Because the leg kick plays such an important part in breaststroke it should be practised more by breaststrokers than other strokes specialists will practise their kicks. From a position in which the legs are straight out and level with the toes pointed the knees are bent and the feet drawn up to the buttocks. Some swimmers can actually touch their heels against their bottom, they are so flexible. Once the feet are thus drawn up they are turned outwards so that the toes point out and the heels in. The propulsive part of the leg action now follows, the feet kicking powerfully and quickly outwards, and just before the legs are fully straightened coming together. The kick is completed with an extension of the feet so that the legs and feet are in a streamlined position.

A common fault with many swimmers is that instead of drawing their feet up to their bottom just below the surface they pull their knees up in front of their hips. As a result of this fault they retard their forward movement and can kick only weakly. They also push their hips onto or even above the surface, and this habit must be avoided at all costs.

The breath on breaststroke is taken on every stroke, and it is not worth practising any variations on this rhythm. The best spot in the stroke to breathe is when the hands are spinning in to the chest. At this point your pull will have lifted your shoulders slightly so it is an easy matter to bring the mouth clear of the water and inhale. There is no need to raise yourself more than is absolutely necessary, and in calm water you can even leave your chin in the water. In training, with choppier water, you will come out higher, but in the ideal conditions of competition, which is what you should be thinking about, a high position is unnecessary.

The co ordination of the arms to the legs and of the breathing in breaststroke varies slightly from swimmer to swimmer, and there is no need to copy one particular method slavishly. Ideally the arms should be pulling as the legs are stretched kick, and conversely the legs should be kicking as the arms are stretching forward. The breath may be taken at any point while the arms are pulling, and there are swimmers who breathe early in the pull and those who breathe right at the end. Both are equally correct, but it is incorrect for the breath to be taken as the arms are going forward and the legs kicking.

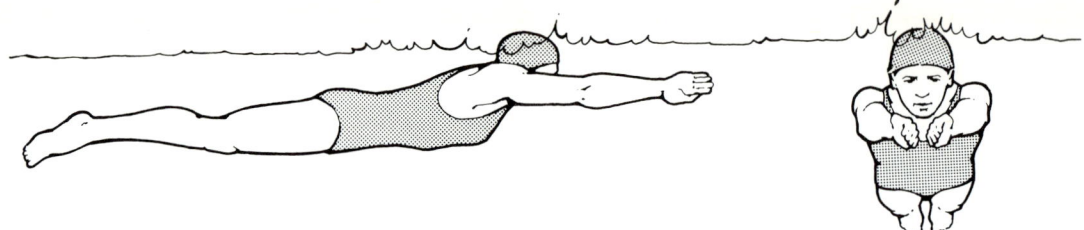

1. The streamlined stretch layout desirable for a fraction of a second in any breaststroke.

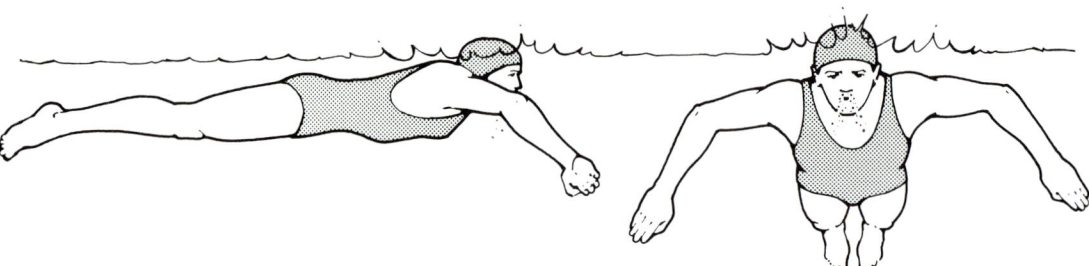

2. The first part of the arm pull as they pull back and wide with the elbows high and bent. The legs have not moved at this point.

3. The hands scoop in under the chest as the pull is completed and the head lifted for the in breath. The legs begin to draw up to the buttocks.

4. The feet are coming up quickly as the underwater recovery of the arms is made. The breath completed, the head is lowered—but not below the surface.

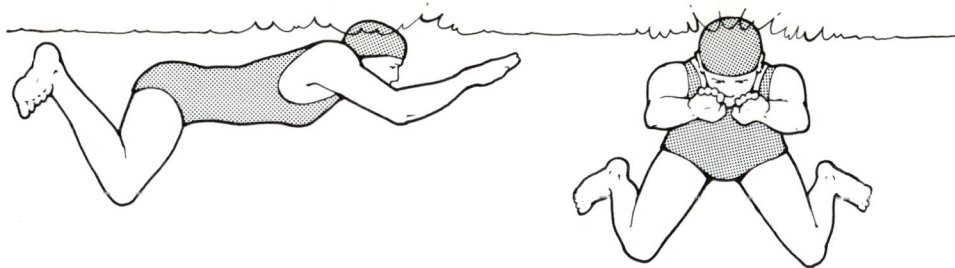

5. As soon as the legs have drawn up to their maximum they kick back, out, and round, with the feet turned outwards. The recovery of the arms is almost . . .

6. . . . complete as the feet finish their kick by coming together and resuming the streamlined position shown in Figure 1.

The temptation to look around during a breaststroke race is almost irresistible to many. Be strong, however, and swim your own race.

The photographer's natural shot of breaststroke: Graham Smith at the moment of inhaling at the end of the arm pull. Smith dominated the 1978 Commonwealth Games, winning six gold medals, including two for breaststroke.

Five Points for Breaststrokers

1. Spin the hands in at the end of the pull so that your hands complete the pull correctly and go straight on into the recovery.
2. Breathe while your arms are spinning at the end of the pull.
3. Bring your feet up quickly to begin the kick and keep them near the surface.
4. Complete the kick with your feet stretched out behind you: if you do you will have kicked correctly and you will be well streamlined.
5. Complete the pull with your arms stretched in front of you. There is little scope in the breaststroke arm pull so it is important to use every possible inch.

Breaststroke Training and Practices

Breaststroke is like backstroke in that even specialist breaststroke swimmers will not swim a great deal of their own stroke in training. But as there is little transfer of skill from the other strokes to breaststroke, especially with the kick, the breaststroker will often find himself carrying out his own special practices. For example, there will be roughly twice as much kicking as with the other strokes, and a good deal of full stroke swimming at something less than top speed.

1. Kicking with kicking boards is perhaps the most basic and common breaststroke drill, and it

Kicking with a large float. The different numbers and sizes of float provide the swimmer with small and subtle changes of stress in this training drill.

is beneficial, as it was in the front crawl, to vary the use of one, two, or three boards. Kicking may be done slowly, with concentration on the two essential features of the kick—the bend of the knee up to the buttocks and the full extension at the end of the kick—or it may be done at speed in sets of short repeats, such as 4 x 50 metres.

2. Kicking without the board is just a little harder than kicking with the board, especially if you do it without moving your hands at all and keep your finger-tips out of the water. An alternative drill, with a different emphasis altogether, is to kick with your hands by your sides, trying to touch your heels with your fingers each time you kick. The idea of this drill is not to get to the other end of the pool as quickly as possible but to improve the range of movement in the legs.

3. Kicking on the back is a useful occasional variation, especially if you are having trouble with the kick, as it enables you to see what your legs are doing. Keep your hips well up to the surface and your knees below it: draw your feet up to your buttocks without dropping your hips and watch them sweep round and back to the finishing position.

4. Pulling: it's not usually necessary for breaststrokers to do much pulling as in this aspect of the stroke there is plenty of carry-over from the crawl strokes, but some pulling, with or without some support for the legs, is necessary if only to encourage the breaststroker to concentrate on what precisely his or her arms are doing. The emphasis should be on the scooping action of the hands and the stretch forward.

5. Putting the stroke together. Just for fun try some of these drills as variations on the full stroke.

(a) swim with alternate single arm pulls;
(b) vary the timing by taking two arm pulls to each leg kick, or two leg kicks to each arm pull; or make the ratio three to one;
(c) swim with as long a glide as possible—but

The start is a crucial moment in any race, and the underwater stroke makes it more so in breaststroke. David Wilkie here seems to be streamlining himself while he is still in the air.

don't vary any of the other movements of the stroke;
(d) butterfly-breaststroke. When the butterfly stroke was first developed the breaststroke swimmers brought their arms forward above the water in the butterfly manner. Though the butterfly-breaststroke is now obsolete as a racing stroke it is still a useful breaststroke practice.

The Start

The start and the turn in breaststroke are two areas in which many races have been won and lost. In the Olympic Games there is little difference between the swimmers, so little advantage is to be gained. But at lower levels those swimmers who have perfected their starts and turns will have a considerable edge on their rivals. And the more elementary the level of swimming the worse, as a rule, will be the standard of starting and turning.

It is important to remember that the rules allow you to take one complete stroke under water at the start and the turn.

Breaststroke races start with a dive, and whether your preferred start is a grab or a wind up it will be necessary for you to enter the water

Below *Touch at the turn and the finish with both hands simultaneously and at the same level, keeping shoulders square. Push off flat, too.* Right *After the touch tuck your body up small to make the turn as quick as possible.* Below right *Towards the end of the push-off phase, kick and reach for the surface. One complete stroke underwater is permitted at the start, and after each turn.*

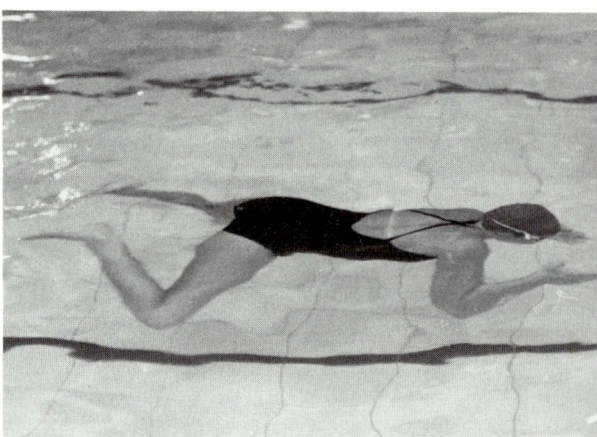

smoothly. This is not so important in front crawl or butterfly, but in breaststroke you want to travel under water fast, so don't slow yourself down with a flat dive. Instead, enter the water at a slight angle with your hands together—preferably with thumbs interlocked—and your feet stretched behind you. Travel 1 to 2 feet below the surface, and when you feel yourself slow down make a wide arm pull with straight arms, out and back until your hands come against your thighs. This pull should be flat so that you don't unconsciously make an illegal dolphin kick with your legs, which should remain still. With the pull you will accelerate, and when you begin to slow once more quickly bring your hands under your chest, draw your legs up, and kick for the surface, stretching your arms forward. Remember, you may not begin to take a second arm pull until your head has broken the surface.

The best breaststroke starts combine a long underwater travel with speed. It is no use going a long distance slowly, but on the other hand there is everything to be said for getting as much out of the start as you can. To be sure that your start is as good as you can make it, practise it every time you dive in to start swimming breaststroke.

The Turn

When finishing a length on breaststroke, coming into a turn or the finish, you must touch the wall with both hands on the same level and at the same time. You should also still be swimming quite flat, with your shoulders level. Many experienced swimmers have been disqualified for breaking these simple rules.

At the turn, after touching in accordance with the rules, bring your inside arm down under the water and your outside arm round above the water and push off smoothly about a foot below the surface. (If you spin clockwise your left arm will be the outside arm and your right arm the inside arm.) Push off perfectly flat and from here on the movements are the same as for the start, though you will obviously not be able to travel so far out of the turn as you can at the start.

Butterfly

There is a myth which is believed in badly-informed circles that the butterfly is a tough stroke to swim, a stroke that only exceptionally strong and fit people can do. Go to any inter-club meet and you will see swimmers who have either been badly taught or who have learnt badly with poor strokes struggling to swim even one length of butterfly. This sort of thing gets a natural and good looking stroke a bad name. But see butterfly being swum by somebody who has learnt the stroke well and you will be looking at something completely different, and when performed by such swimmers, who have found how to make the water help them, butterfly is a free-flowing and spectacular sight.

Butterfly is a stroke in which, in the best performers, technique and power are combined. You may get so far without strength, but nowhere at all without a basically correct technique.

The Stroke

Like breaststroke, from which it evolved, butterfly is a symmetrical stroke. The arms should move at the same time and make identical movements, and likewise the legs should kick in unison. And just as in breaststroke the touches at the turn and finish must be made with both hands simultaneously and at the same level, so it is in butterfly.

The body in butterfly should be kept always perfectly flat on the breast with no movement to either side. This fact apart there is no single position, as the angle and depth of the body is constantly changing as the stroke cycle progresses. The body, in fact, acts not so much as a fixed platform for the arms and legs, as it does in, say, front crawl, but has a definite role to play, and if you try to keep your body perfectly still you will not be able to swim the stroke properly at all. The stroke is sometimes known as the 'dolphin butterfly', and this name conveys exactly what the butterfly is about: long undulating movements of the body performed smoothly, gracefully and powerfully, finishing with a whip-like kick from the feet. We shall find out more about the body movements as we go on and describe the other aspects of the stroke.

The head in butterfly may be treated as an extension of the body, as the head always leads the body into its undulating 'dolphin' movements, lifting slightly in breathing and leading the body down into the diving part of the stroke. The head should always face the front and is not turned to breathe.

The butterfly arm action has two functions: to provide propulsion and to aid breathing. The hands enter the water in front of the shoulders, and form a position in which the arms are stretched out in front, the head between the arms, the pull should proceed roughly as follows. First the hands begin to move outwards in the same sequence as front crawl—fingers, hands, then arms—feeling the water. When the hands are about 18 inches to 2 feet apart and pulling out and down at angles of about 45 degrees the elbows should be bent, the hands pulled inwards until they almost touch just beneath the shoulders. It is at this point that most swimmers begin to lift their heads to inhale. After this 'pull' phase of the arm pull, the 'push' phase is reached and the hands continue to follow through as the arms straighten until they slice out of the water just behind and slightly wide of the hip bone.

In no swimming stroke is it possible or desirable to pull the arms through in a perfectly straight line, and from underwater observations butterfly swimmers appear to use one of two basic variations in pulling patterns. The first is called the 'hour glass pull', in which the pull begins with the hands a little more than shoulder width apart. The hands then move slightly outwards and then inwards until the finger-tips almost touch below the shoulders, and then they push out strongly out and back. The second variation is called the 'keyhole pull', and in this the hands enter the water very close together, pull outwards (as we described earlier) and then inwards, pushing out and back to complete the pulling phase. The essential difference between

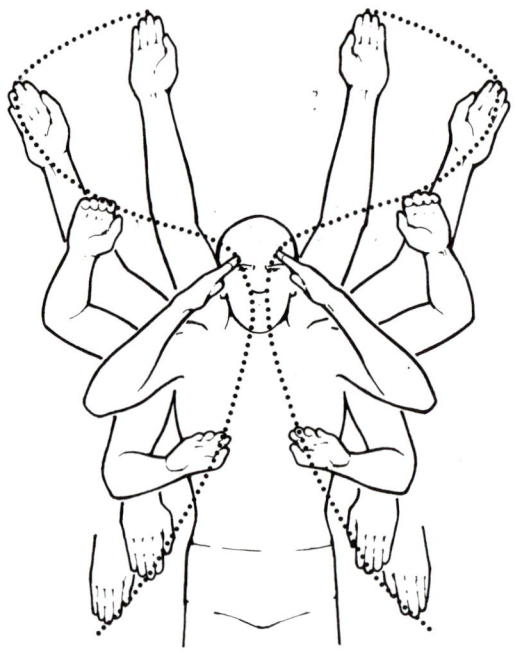

The butterfly pull seen from below. Notice the hand entry at shoulder width, the outward and then inward pull until the hands almost touch below the top of the chest, and finally the long outward push phase.

these two styles is in the entry position of the hands. It is not important for you to analyse your stroke minutely and to follow either style rigidly, because for one thing you will almost certainly have an in-between style anyway, but it is vital that you realize that you can't pull back in a straight line.

Once the hands have been flipped clear, little fingers first, of the water by the hips at the end of the pull the recovery phase begins. The arms are swung forward sideways across the water, as relaxed as possible, until the hands can enter the

Mark Spitz on the way to one of his seven gold medals at Munich in 1972. Ten years of preparation led to Spitz's becoming the most successful swimmer in history with gold medals coming from two butterfly and two individual freestyle events and three winning relays.

water in front of the shoulders. You should try to make the hands enter thumbs first, as this will put your arms in the correct and best position to start the pull. The recovery is not made with straight arms, nor is it a double front crawl action, but is somewhere between the two.

We come to the leg action near the end of this analysis, but the leg kick is a vital part of butterfly swimming and links the other parts of the stroke together. It is possible to swim a stroke resembling butterfly without using the legs properly, but to do that is to put yourself at an unnecessary disadvantage. The kick is an extension of the movement of the body, and the whole set of arm–body–leg movements jig-saws together.

There are two leg down-beats to each arm stroke. The first comes as the hands enter and aids the dive down to the catch point where the pull begins. The hips rise in reaction to the downwards movement of the shoulders while the legs kick down to add their momentum to the drive of the hands. As the pull progresses the hips sink slightly and the feet are drawn up to the surface and towards the hips. Towards the end of the push phase of the arm pull, as the arms move upwards there should be a second strong downward leg beat. This kick serves two purposes: it lifts the shoulders to make the recovery easier and to lift the head for the breath, and it also provides a surge to carry the body through the moment when there will be no propulsive movements and the arms are in the air. In fact, at this moment the swimmer is moving at his maximum speed in the stroke. As the arms recover the legs once again rise to be ready to kick as the hands enter. This second kick is the one to accentuate, although the first kick is usually bigger.

We have already described the breathing a little. Inhalation is made when the face is lifted clear of the water during the later stages of the pull and early part of the recovery. As soon as the breath has been taken the head should be dropped so that the chin returns to the chest—so aiding the dive into the catch.

Most swimmers breathe at every other stroke,

1. The hands have just entered ahead of the shoulders and the feet are beginning their big downward kick. The head has dropped, chin to chest, after the breath.

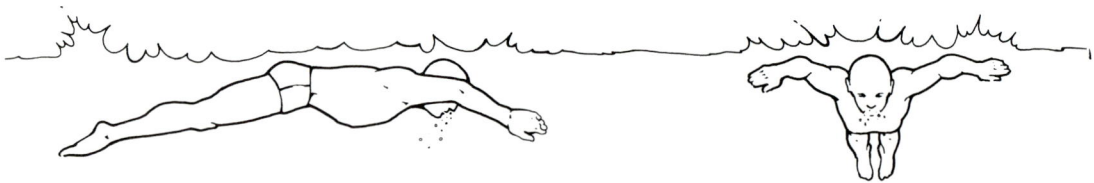

2. Here the hands have made the first, outward, part of the pull while the leg kick has reached its deepest point. Notice the elbows are kept high.

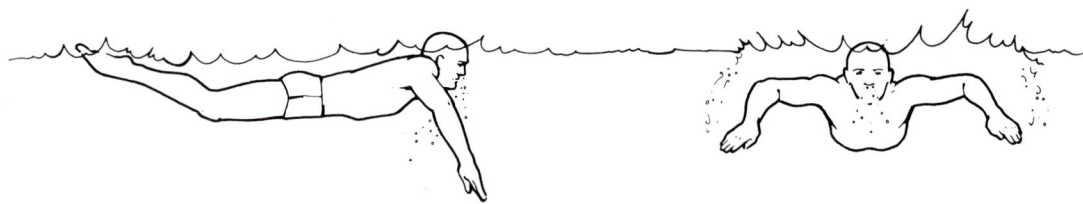

3. The arms are now beginning to pull inwards as the head begins to rise with the shoulders following. The feet lift to balance the head.

4. Halfway through the pull and the hands now almost meet beneath the chest. The head is about to rise for the breath and the feet are ready for the second kick.

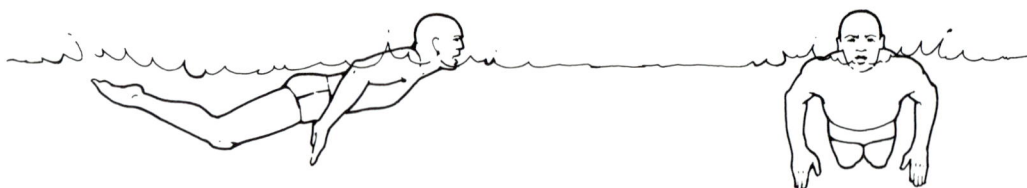

5. The moment of breathing in. The arms are now pushing back and about to slice out while the feet are kicking vigorously downwards to provide speed for the recovery.

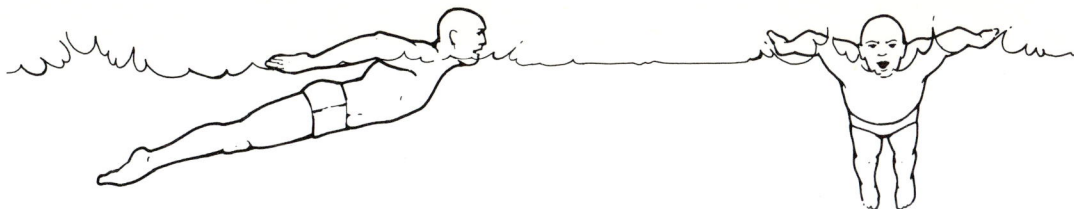

6. The breath is about to be completed as the arms recover above the water and the leg kick is completed.

7. The end of the cycle comes as the head is dropped down and the hands come forward to recommence the stroke as the feet rise once more prior to the kick.

and as this is a stroke in which rhythm is important it is best to stick to this frequency. As your swimming improves you can experiment with swimming two strokes to one breath during the early stages of a race. In general, though, you will find it best at first to stick to one stroke per breath.

An Underwater Stroke

Because we normally see butterfly being swum from the poolside we tend to think of it as a stroke swum along the top of the water. But if you could watch good butterfly swimmers from below the water you would be soon converted to the view

Halfway through the butterfly pull. The hands almost touch as they pull past the shoulders.

that it is mainly an underwater stroke. Viewed from beneath, the swimmer breaks the surface only to breathe and to recover: the remainder of the stroke is performed below the surface. If you want to swim butterfly comfortably and well, you must adjust yourself to this underwater view.

Two Essentials of Successful Butterfly Swimming

1. Dive in and down to start the pull. Three combined movements transform the limp surface butterfly into the graceful dolphin stroke you should aim at. As the hands enter they should drive forwards and downwards. At the same time, as the heads drops down after the breath the chin should be held firm against the chest. And, thirdly, there should be a strong downward leg beat at this point.
2. Explode out at the back of the pull. Too many swimmers stop at the end of the pull and try to start the recovery from scratch. A smooth continuation of movement at this point is essential, and it is aided by the second leg kick which is made just as the pull is being finished.

Butterfly Training and Practices

In the beginning butterfly is tiring, and it is best not to attempt to swim the full stroke for long distances. It is preferable to swim short distances with correct technique rather than longer distances poorly. Many swimmers find it more fun as well as beneficial to combine some of the drills described below with the full stroke. As you become more proficient in this stroke you will be able to cover what had once seemed impossible distances with the full stroke without any loss of technique, and this is a sign of good butterfly.

When you are first learning butterfly, or trying to develop the dolphin technique, you may find it useful to wear flippers occasionally. Flippers accentuate the action of the feet, and not only will you swim faster—always a good thing to do—but you will find yourself feeling the natural urge to include two kicks to each arm pull. Even when you have the stroke 'right' an occasional revision with flippers is helpful.

As well as the timing, some swimmers have trouble controlling their breathing during butterfly, mainly through not knowing quite when to lift their heads to breathe. A useful drill for a starter in the stroke is to simply 'bob' up and down in the water, breathing in when your face is out of the water and breathing out under water. Do this in deep water slowly. Progress from this to kicking under water and breathing after making a short breaststroke pull to bring yourself to the surface. After mastering this it is a simple step to substitute a full butterfly arm stroke for the breaststroke, though the exercise is still based on underwater dolphin kicking.

Kicking drills in butterfly are complicated by, as we have already discovered, the continually changing body position. For this reason it is not desirable always to use kicking boards when practising the leg action. But kicking is still the time to think about the proper positioning of the legs—together—and the feet—with the toes turned slightly inward. Possible variations on kicking drills are as follows:

1. Kicking holding the poolside: a nice way of getting the initial feel of the stroke.
2. Kicking with the hands by the side. In this drill the major movements come, as they do in the full stroke, from the hips. You should be able to feel the legs and feet following the up and down hip movement.
3. Kicking on the side. If on the right side, hold the right arm in front and let the left hand trail, or vice versa. You will be able to see that the legs actually kick backwards and not just sideways (or, in the prone position, downwards).
4. Kicking on the front, hands extended. If you can kick continuously with your hands extended and the fingers on the surface without having to use your hands for support, your kick has come on very well.

Kicking on the side is one of the most valuable butterfly drills. If nothing else, it makes you think of what your feet actually do!

Single-arm butterfly. Right *Holding the free arm still in front, the swimmer recovers his pulling arm as high and as straight as possible and breathes to the side.* Left *Single arm butterfly. With the free arm held by the side the swimmer now breathes to the front.*

5. Single-arm butterfly. This drill is for use by butterfly swimmers of all standards. Holding one arm quite still out in front of you swim the full stroke using one arm only. Recover the moving arm straight and as high in the air as possible while breathing to the *side* of the recovering arm. Swimmers who have trouble getting the two-beat timing of the full stroke sometimes acquire it unconsciously with this drill. Remember still to dive in with the entering hand.

6. Variations of single-arm butterfly include the use of alternate arms, or a combination of single-arm and full-stroke. For instance: left, right, both arms, and so on. Alternatively, swim alternate lengths on single-arm butterfly as three length (or width) sets of single-arm (left), single-arm (right), full stroke, and so on.

Single-arm butterfly can also be swum with the resting arm held by the side. In this case take the breath to the front. Not so many variations are possible with this style, but there is still a great carry-over into the full stroke.

7. Diving butterfly. In the early days of butterfly swimming, in the 1950s when even international swimmers were hardly as well trained as today's age-groupers, it was not uncommon for top swimmers to disappear under the surface to propel themselves with large dolphin leg kicks, coming up only to breathe. Try this, taking as many leg kicks as possible before your breath runs out and you have to come up. Alternatively, once you are used to the stroke you can start a swim (in training only, mind) with the diving stroke and reduce the number of kicks per arm stroke until you end up on the final section of your swim with the racing timing of two kicks to one arm stroke.

Kicking butterfly underwater to get the feel of the undulating dolphin movement.

Breathing Patterns

There are two basic patterns of breathing in butterfly. The simplest is to breathe on every stroke, and this is how we would encourage all young swimmers to start. Later, try breathing every other stroke, especially at the start of a race. However, if you are caught up in a very short race of 50 metres or less, it may be worth breathing as little as possible, provided you don't let your anxiety to swim fast come between you and the stroke. Not all fast movements in swimming actually produce extra speed.

The Start and Turn

The butterfly start and turn are, unlike those of the other strokes, relatively simple affairs. At the start you can use either form of stance—grab or wind up—to get into the water, and once you are in the rules allow you to take as many leg kicks as you like before surfacing. But most swimmers find they swim faster times if they stay below the water for as little as possible at the start of a race or at the turn.

The butterfly turn is like the breaststroke turn in that you must touch the wall with both hands simultaneously and on the same level. So keep your shoulders level until you've actually hit the wall. Likewise, you must push off perfectly level once your feet have left the wall. From touch to push-off you must simply tuck up and turn round as you do in breaststroke, as quickly as possible.

Remember that the rules say that the arms must recover above the water. This means that any forward movement of the arms relative to the body must be done above the surface. It is always tempting if you come up short at a turn or the finish to bring yourself in to the wall with a little breaststroke arm pull. If you do and the judges are doing their jobs properly you must be disqualified, wherever you finished and whatever time you did, because you will have violated the rules of the stroke. So judge your approach to the wall so that you hit it perfectly, especially at the finish where it might be the difference between winning and losing. If you do misjudge your approach and are left with an awkward gap between your hands and the wall and it is not possible to take a further arm stroke simply kick into the wall keeping your hands still in front of you.

Below *Keep your head as low as you dare and breathe as close to the water as possible in butterfly. Gabrielle Wuschek (East Germany), third in the 1975 world championships.*

British international Mark Thorne gives some idea of the power generated by men butterfly swimmers.

A butterfly swimmer must have flexible shoulders to perform the stroke properly, especially the arm recovery.

Water Polo

A team game for the water, water polo was developed in Britain in the nineteenth century. Its name implies that the game was once linked with the kind of polo played on horseback, and although some early prints show a game being played on barrels made up to look like horses the game soon evolved into a handling code with more in common with land handball than the polo favoured by the royal family.

In essence water polo is a team game played between teams of seven players, the object of the game being to score as many goals as possible. The first rules roughly resembling those in use today were drawn up in the Midlands in 1884, with the English governing body following suit in 1885. Many changes have been made since those days, but the basic idea of a ball-throwing game in which to score goals is the prime object has remained. Most of the changes have been intended to improve the game for players and spectators, and each successive change has made the game better. Although some of the roughness which once typified water polo has gone, the essential character of the game as a sport for strong swimmers who can handle a ball well has been preserved.

Water polo in the 1890s, soon after the first rules were implemented which gave the game its modern shape. An illustration from The Badminton Library book Swimming, *1893.*

A packed zonal defence presents even the best attackers with problems.

At one time British water polo led the world, and British teams won the Olympic title in 1900, 1908, 1912 and 1920. Since that time the British game has gone into something of a decline and has been overtaken by well-organized state-run teams from Eastern Europe. Britain has given way to Hungary in the leadership of world water polo, and Hungarian sides were Olympic winners in 1932, 1936, 1952, 1956, 1964 and 1976. The USSR and Yugoslavia have also won Olympic titles in recent Games.

Despite this, it is difficult to find a part of Britain in which water polo is not played. The strongest club teams tend to come from the big city areas—London, Manchester, Birmingham, Liverpool—but there are significant outposts at Cheltenham, Newport (Monmouthshire), Weston-super-Mare, and elsewhere. But that is for the enthusiast. For the swimmer just starting out and wanting to know more about the game there is sure to be a club fairly close at hand where he can learn.

Water polo is traditionally a game for men and boys, and there are very few teams for women or girls. Most games are open to players of all ages, and the average age of a water polo team is considerably more than that of a swimming team. Players can continue to play at a high standard for much longer than swimmers competing at national or even at county level, and very often the older players, aged between 30 and 40, and even older, are the best. It is difficult, and in many people's opinion unwise, for even well-built boys of 14 and 15 to try to compete with mature players on equal terms. But many clubs run junior teams through which an aspiring player can learnt the finer points of the game without being exposed too early. The commonest age-group in water polo is under 18, and many counties and areas run league and knock-out cup competitions for this group. An age range less commonly catered for is under 16, though there are English club championships for under 16 and under 18 teams. In some clubs where water polo has a strong following even younger teams are run on a regular basis, though their activities are naturally limited through a shortage of opposition and of pool time. So if your club does not run junior teams it is not necessarily through lack of interest!

Water polo is played between teams of 11 players each, 7 of whom may be in the water at any time. Substitutions are made after a goal has been scored and between periods, there being four periods of five minutes each actual playing time (the timekeeper's watch being stopped while the ball is dead). A team consists of field players and a goalkeeper, all of whom may change positions and be substituted.

The game starts with a toss up for ends, the winner of the toss usually choosing to attack the deep end goal (if there is one) during the final period. The game commences with the players lined up along their goal line: the referee throws the ball into the centre of the field, and the players sprint for the ball. The field players, who may not walk, or stand to play the ball, attempt to score goals by throwing the ball. They may not punch the ball or handle it with both hands simultaneously. The goalkeeper is exempt from the bans on standing or punching.

There are two grades of foul. Minor fouls, for which the penalty is a free throw to the opposition include: holding onto the side of the pool, walking, taking the ball under, playing the ball with both hands simultaneously, to simulate being fouled, going within 2 metres of the opponent's goal without the ball, for a team to retain possession of the ball for more than 35 seconds without shooting. Major fouls, for which the penalty is to be ordered out of the water for 45 seconds or for which a penalty throw is awarded if the foul is committed within the opposition's 4-metre area, include: holding or sinking an opponent who does not have the ball, repeatedly committing an ordinary foul, interfering with the taking of a free throw, arguing with the referee. A player committing three major fouls is automatically excluded from the game, though he may be substituted. For an act of brutality, such as punching or kicking an opponent, a player is sent from the water permanently without substitution.

You will see from this that contact between players is a part of water polo, and strong tackling is one of its features. Fouls resulting from incorrect or unfair tackles are a common sight.

The goalkeeper, expecting a hard flat shot, may be deceived by a lob. The keeper here is treading water in a pool over six feet deep.

But in general the game is exceptionally clean, compared with football or rugby, because players who commit fouls are readily penalized and sent from the water to cool off. A good team manager will also substitute a player whose temper is fraying. Consequently there are very few injuries in water polo.

The general qualities of water polo are similar to those of other team games. Team work is of the essence and the brilliant player who is continually sent out or who shoots indiscriminately is of no use to a team. It is also a game which will last you for very many years, something speed swimming, regrettably, does not.

There are some swimming coaches who disapprove of their young swimmers taking part in water polo. The main drawbacks as they see it are that water polo is time consuming, that playing it regularly disrupts swimming training, and it is sad to say that hard training is not a feature of many water polo players. However, for all but the very ambitious swimmer water polo is an excellent game that will give you many years of enjoyment and friendship.

Marking tight. These white defenders will try to prevent the blue attackers from getting clear while at the same time try not to be penalised for impeding or holding.

Complete ball control and powerful shooting—both made more easily attainable by the new composition ball—are features of water polo at its best.

Long-distance Swimming

Long-distance swimming is not only a branch of swimming but a sport in its own right, and many speed swimmers—those whose activities are normally confined to the pool—have found long-distance events an entertaining and invigorating variation on the usual round of sprint swims. For the champion distance swimmer there is always the challenge of competing in a race in company with some of all sport's finest endurance athletes, and for the novice or the plodder who never wins there is the challenge and satisfaction of finishing swims which are a severe test of character and fitness. The long-distance fraternity also regards its competitions as fun, and the swimmer who just finishes is held in as high regard as the one who finishes first.

British long-distance swimming is co-ordinated centrally by the British Long Distance Swimming Association (BLDSA), a body formed in 1956. The BLDSA co-ordinates most of the major amateur long-distance swimming races in Britain as well as providing an information service on events not under its direct jurisdiction. The BLDSA also keeps records of individual swims, as does the Channel Swimming Association for the English Channel crossing.

Although there is no 'centre' of long-distance swimming in Britain any more than there is a centre of speed swimming, it is fair to say that the general focus of the sport is in the north of England where there are more suitable stretches of open water, especially in the Lake District. But the swimmer from the south or from Scotland should not despair, as there are events held all over the country.

Most long-distance swims are for open category swimmers, those of any age. However, the BLDSA organizes a series of Junior swims, restricted to boys and girls between the ages of 12 and 16 years. In all BLDSA races, though not in all privately organized events, competitors must produce a recent medical certificate of fitness, and during each swim each swimmer is under the control of an experienced pilot-lifesaver whose responsibility it is to see that the swimmer follows the correct course and does not get into difficulties. If a swimmer is suffering physical distress the pilot-lifesaver will stop him or her from continuing. This official's word is final, and consequently the BLDSA races have a fine safety record. Other BLDSA races are open to swimmers over the age of 16, and they are subject to the same regulations. Swimmers younger than 16 are excluded.

The lure of long-distance swimming has always existed, and the swimming heroes of antiquity were known more for their endurance than their speed. The great modern inspirer of long-distance swimming is, of course, Captain Matthew Webb, the Shropshire-born ship's officer who made the first swim across the English Channel, from England to France in 21

The start of the Lake Bala one-way race. Canoes are necessary to keep up with the faster swimmers.

A contemporary print shows Captain Webb landing in France. CSA rules now insist that a swimmer must walk unassisted beyond the high-water mark.

hours 45 minutes on the 24th of August 1875. Though it was many years before Webb's achievement was emulated and longer before his time was beaten he is recognized as the first great modern distance swimmer. Even today, despite improved navigation and training methods, to complete the swim is a marvellous achievement and the product of many months of hard training and preparation. The record for the fastest crossing is now held by an Egyptian, Nasser El Shazley (8 hours 45 minutes on the 21st of August 1977), and the youngest swimmer to get across is an English boy, David Morgan, who was aged 13 years and 5 months when he swam from England to France in 11 hours 51 minutes on the 26th of July 1977.

Although Webb swam the Channel using breaststroke, most swimmers today use front crawl in long-distance swims, although it is a longer, slower, and smoother stroke than that used by sprinters. Economy of effort aimed at consistent progress over a long period is the

Kevin Murphy has been the outstanding distance swimmer of the 1970s in European waters, and is one of a number of people who never made speed swimmers but went on to excel in the longer events.

Inshore (now a 2-mile indoor opener for the season); Pickmere Lake, Cheshire (2 miles); Wharfe river, Otley, Yorkshire (1 mile); Sandsend to Whitby, Yorkshire (3 miles); Derwentwater, Cumbria (2 miles); Jersey, Channel Islands (3 miles); Langold Lake, Derbyshire (2 miles); Waterloo Lake, Leeds (2 miles); Lake Bala, North Wales (3 miles). In addition to these there are many swims at coastal resorts such as the pier-to-pier swims at Brighton and Southsea. There is certainly plenty to choose from and if your prospects of getting far in sprint swimming look slim, long-distance swimming could give you a new, fresh and, maybe, successful future.

Thirteen-year-old Abla Khairy of Egypt being greased up prior to her 1974 English Channel swim. At that time she was the Channel's youngest conqueror.

keynote. But in the junior swims, especially those held in calm water, there need be no dropping away from 'correct' technique for the young swimmer who need not fear that his other swimming activities will suffer if he takes part in open water races. In rough water, or in the sea, a more robust stroke is needed, it is true, but that does not concern us here. But although the most common stroke used is front crawl there are a number of successful long-distance swimmers who swim breaststroke, and swim results often list those who swim breaststroke separately.

The age-group swimmer who decides to have a go at long-distance swimming will be unwise if he or she drops out of conventional sprint swimming training. Much training is today geared to the longer events in the pool as they become more widespread in county championships. Long swims in short indoor pools are mindlessly monotonous if swum regularly, and the variation in distance and stress in a club training programme is in itself valuable. Occasional longer swims are certainly helpful, as are practice open-air swims, but the best training for long-distance swimming is the race itself. The senior swimmers recognize this and their year's programme starts with quite short swims and builds up to a climax in August, while the sea is still warm enough for Channel swims in September and October.

In 1978 the BLDSA programme of Junior swims included the following events: Morecambe

Synchronized Swimming

The sport of synchronized swimming is difficult to describe simply as it involves so many different swimming skills. It has been defined as 'any form of movement in water in which the swimmer synchronizes with music or with other swimmers'. If speed swimming can be compared with track running, then synchronized swimming, or 'synchro' as it is often called, can best be compared with gymnastics or ice skating. It is a skilful art in which competitors perform movements for their aesthetic appeal.

Synchro is a water sport which has evolved from water ballet. The first performances bore little resemblance to modern synchro, but its first successful exponent was the Australian Annette Kellerman who gave swimming demonstrations in White City Park, Chicago, in 1905. She exhibited the then approved styles of swimming and some 'fantastic stunts—porpoise swimming and the like', to quote her own words.

Water ballet was popularized in the 1940s by Esther Williams, especially in films. Synchro caught on in North America, and exhibitions were held in Europe. Then, in 1958, the Metropolitan Diving School team entered the 'Festival of Europe', having been inspired by a travelling American group, the Athens Water Follies. But organized competitions in Britain had to wait until 1969, when the first international trials were held for a competition against France in Paris.

From this date we can trace a healthy growth of synchro in Britain, so much so that Britain is now the leading European nation and ranks fourth in the world behind the USA, Canada and Japan.

Synchronized swimming is traditionally a sport for girls, although some clubs accept boy members. The basic skills involve general watermanship, and these can certainly be enjoyed by both boys and girls. These skills provide a sound basis for all water-based activities. Competitive work, however, relies on a grace which is often lacking in boys. Synchro was once a sport for ex-competitive swimmers and divers who wanted to stay in swimming without

The Reading Royals team demonstrating their skills in coordination. The minimum number in a synchro team is four, and bonus points are to be gained for further team members up to a maximum of eight.

Above *An underwater shot of the dolphin, foot-first, bent-knee movement at Santa Clara, home of the world team champions for 1978.*

Opposite above *The ballet leg stunt during a duet competition. Simultaneous movements and an uncanny degree of understanding are essential in the duet and team events.*

Opposite below *Britain's effort at synchronized swimming has been rewarded with a world fourth place ranking, a position confirmed in all three events at the 1978 world championships. Jenny Lane was fourth in the individual.*

the strenuous training demanded by those activities, but it has changed greatly and many girls start out as synchro swimmers. Successful synchro swimmers put in as much training as speed swimmers.

Training is divided into stamina, figure and routine work in the pool and strength and flexibility work on dry land. Stamina is essential for performing a good five-minute routine. Strength is required to hold the body in set positions in the water. And flexibility is required if the figures are to be performed with clean line and design.

A synchro competition is divided into two categories. The first part is the figure section in which all competitors perform a set number of compulsory figures. Usually six are required: but for local competitions this number may vary. Each competitor performs alone, wearing a plain dark costume, and is marked by a panel of judges who look for clear definition of each section and a controlled performance. This section is very repetitive, and spectator interest is limited. But the routine section, in which the swimmer may wear an appropriate costume, is an excellent spectator sport.

The routine section comes in three forms: solo, duet and team (four to eight swimmers making up a team). Each routine may last up to five minutes and is marked on variety, difficulty, interpretation of music, manner of presentation and synchronization with music and the other swimmers. The pool pattern is also marked, and competitors should use as much of the allocated space as possible. Judges must consider all these points and then give a mark out of 10, using one decimal place. The music chosen by the competitors is usually non-vocal and instantly recognizable.

The 'fan' position from the Reading Royals. It is maintained for a few seconds by quiet hand swirling movements; the team will then break and re-emerge in a quite different formation.

Synchro relies on a sound knowledge of the basic swimming strokes and these should be well established before a swimmer attempts to join a synchro club. Clubs specializing in this sport are found in most parts of the country. The strokes used in synchro are similar to the racing strokes, but they are swum for effect, not speed, and adapted so that the swimmer can see the other swimmers (and be seen) and so that she can hear the music. For the greatest effect the body is held well up in the water, the legs used for propulsion, and the arms mainly for effect and balance—a very different emphasis from the racing strokes. But most swimmers can adapt from one to the other, and some of the most successful synchro swimmers have also been international speed swimmers.

The most important skill that the synchro swimmer has to learn is sculling. This is a method of propelling or supporting the body using the arms only. The hands move away from and towards the body describing an elongated figure of eight, with the little finger raised and leading on the outward movement and the thumb raised and leading on the inward. These movements must be made smoothly and are used throughout most of the figures.

There are three different types of routine—formation swimming, floating patterns and stroke and figure routines. The first two are seen mainly in displays whereas the third is used for competitive work. Formation swimming is essential for all synchro swimmers as it helps to develop synchronization with other swimmers, moving with music, team work and discipline, all of which are necessary for future competitive work. Floating patterns are surface formations performed by two or more swimmers. The success of such team routines relies on the swimmers' ability to float, to support themselves by sculling and to support each other by mutually supportive grips. By sculling, the swimmers can then form and change formation giving an attractive kaleidoscopic effect.

As you will have gathered from this chapter, synchronized swimming is a sport in its own right with a very different outlook to speed swimming, and in this space we have done little more than outline its scope without going into too much detail. But if you are interested try to see it locally. If you try it you will find it as rewarding as any sport can be.

Land Conditioning

The phrase 'land conditioning' covers all manner of activities in which swimmers take part on dry land with a view to improving their performance in the water. Some of them are very general, and contribute to the swimmer's all-round athletic ability. Others are quite specific: they are intended to lead to an improvement in one aspect of the swimmer's technique.

Most young swimmers, certainly those still at school, will already take part in a number of different sport which are organized at school and which contribute to their general education as well as improving their physical fitness. These include team games such as rugby, soccer and basketball and individual sports such as running and possibly cycling. Girls tend not to be included in some of these pursuits and often shy away from those they can take part in, and as a result some young girl swimmers are terribly weak. But there is little doubt that if two swimmers are equal in ability and train equally hard in the water but one takes part in a wide range of sports on land and the other does not, the one who neglects this aspect of his or her education will be the poorer swimmer.

Land conditioning is an integral part of the training programmes of many top swimmers, and few if any can reach the top of the sport without some additional training out of the water. For the swimmer there are four main areas of fitness to be considered: skill—the actual movements of swimming which can be practised only in the water; strength—which may be built up or enhanced by many land activities, notably weight training, pulley weights, isometrics, body weight exercises and cord or elastic pulling, endurance—physical stamina which can be improved by circuit training and running, and mobility—an often neglected aspect of fitness which needs no special equipment. Because this book is not written for those swimmers (or their parents) who are already in the advanced swimming competitions, a detailed account of all the possible exercises included in this list is not necessary. But a brief description of some of the more practicable activities may be useful.

Of the exercises designed to increase strength, body weight exercises and pulley or cord pulling are the most commonly used by swimmers. Weight training with heavy weights is, to our minds, unnecessary for the swimmer of county standard. Body weight exercises are those in which the swimmer will use only his or her own weight to provide resistance. Press-ups are the most well-known exercise in this group, with trunk curls or sit-ups coming a close second. Press-ups, of course, improve the strength of the shoulders and arms, trunk curls the condition of the stomach muscles. Canoes, or back lifts, exercise the long muscles of the back. Squat jumps, squat thrusts and burpees are valuable conditioners of the upper leg and stomach. Variation can be brought into these exercises by performing them in different positions (e.g. to vary the height of the feet in press-ups and the degree of lift in trunk curls) or in different numbers (e.g. to do three sets of 10 press-ups one day, two of 15 the next, one of 30 another, and so on).

Pulleys and cord work are valuable as the movements closely follow those of the arm action in swimming, though not precisely. Generally light weights or resistances are used, and the number of movements or repetitions is high. There are various commercial machines on the market, but thick (well-fastened) elastic is equally suitable, and so is lifting a weight attached to a cord run through a pulley.

Weight training is a science of its own and should not be embarked on without close supervision. Some young boys, though, enjoy weight lifting for its own sake and there is little doubt in our minds that a suitable programme of weight lifting coupled with flexibility exercises can do little but good, provided of course the main object of the exercise—to swim better and faster—is kept in mind.

Endurance training on the land is built in to a

number of activities, and a normal schoolchild should have little difficulty in finding out about them. The most obvious and common of the endurance exercises is running, and some successful swimmers have gone into running as an exercise in a big way. Longer steady runs will improve the athlete's respiratory efficiency, which is a short way of saying it will improve the pumping efficiency of the heart (which is a muscle) and the absorption of oxygen into the blood stream in the lungs. Circuit training, in which a series of different exercises is gone through at speed for a certain time or for a set number of movements is another (indoor) method of building up endurance and, at the same time, strength and a certain amount of mobility.

This leads us into an often neglected part of physical fitness, mobility and flexibility. A swimmer needs as much mobility in the joints as possible, as much as a gymnast or a ballet dancer, and it is noticeable that some girls, who take part in those activities, are much more flexible than the stronger muscled boys. Flexibility in a swimmer is necessary for three main reasons. Without a full range of movement in the joints it is impossible to perform certain skills properly. For instance, stiff ankles will lead to poor kicking on all strokes, and lack of shoulder mobility makes it very difficult to swim butterfly or backstroke with the full range or movement, and therefore harder and slower. Muscle injuries are more commonly found in people who lack the full range of arm movement. Lastly, flexible swimmers can exert their full power over a wider range of movement than those who lack mobility.

Building up or maintaining flexibility has more in common with yoga than with the old style or arm and leg flinging, which could in itself lead to injury and more stiffness. Controlled stretching exercises in which the range of movement is progressively increased are the most beneficial. The most important thing that can be said here is that before doing any mobility exercises the swimmer should ensure that he is warm and that his muscles have been warmed up with other exercises, such as a short simple circuit. If you do circuit training or some weight lifting it is important that afterwards you do a few flexibility exercises to prevent your muscles from contracting and restricting your range of movements.

There are two points to emphasize here. First, an adequate indulgence in land conditioning is desirable for swimmers, whatever their speciality or ambition may be. Secondly, land conditioning is only a means to an end, and that must always be to improve the swimmer's performance in the

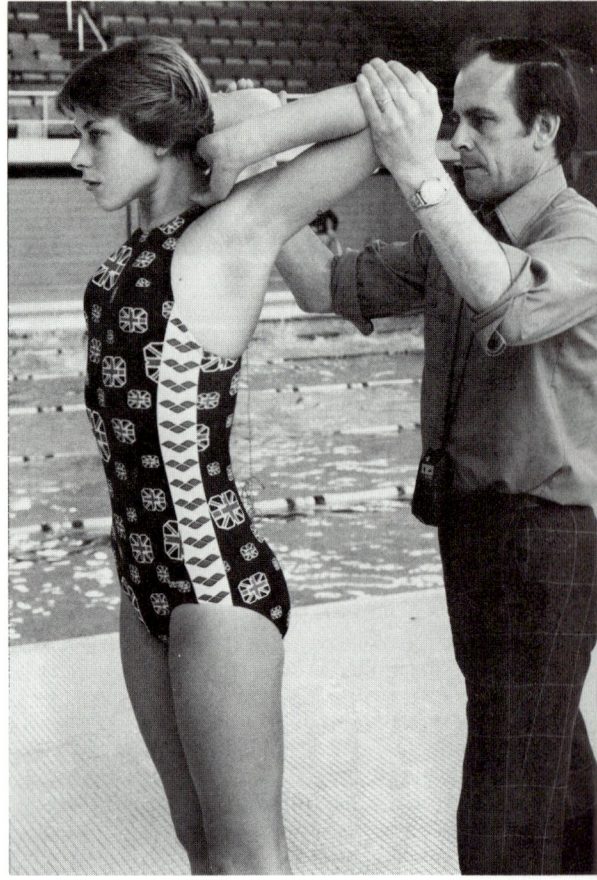

Even the champion swimmer should not neglect the basic mobility routines. Sharron Davies, England's double gold medallist in the 1978 Commonwealth Games, warms up here with her father and coach, Terry. Partner exercises should be done under the strictest supervision.

water. As a last word we should also emphasize that a knowledge of land conditioning cannot be got out of books, and expert advice from a coach or schoolteacher should be sought before you start out.

How Speed Swimming is Organized

The swimmer who is a newly joined member of a club, and even those who have been members for some time, may be only dimly aware of how their sport is organized and what is going on in other places. Such swimmers probably only meet swimmers from other clubs at galas or championship meetings.

The ordinary club swimmer will compete in three types of competition. First, there is the club's own internal racing, normally organized around club championships with prizes or medals at stake. Secondly, there will be inter-club competitions and swimming leagues at which a team from the club will compete against teams selected from other clubs. In some clubs there is strong competition for a place in the club's team. Most swimmers will also have a chance to swim in age-group competitions at county or area level—an English county swimming association's championships being restricted to swimmers from within its boundaries. At such a meet there will be heats and finals of all races, though some longer events will be only heats, with the winners declared on heat times.

In England the level above the county is the district, there being five districts in England—Southern, Western, Midland, Northern and North Eastern, and each district stages its own age-group competitions and championships, entrants for which must have achieved a particular standard.

A swimmer who achieves a standard higher than the district requires may hope to qualify for the national age-group championships. Although these are organized by the English Amateur Swimming Association they are open to swimmers from all over the world.

Age-group competitions are not the only swimming events, and just as a county will have open events in its championship programme, so will a district, and so, naturally, does the national association.

The English ASA, following a pattern set by the Americans and also copied by most other national bodies, holds two championship meetings. In about April comes the Short Course Championships, held in a 25- or 33⅓-metre pool, acting as trials for international competitions to be held in the first part of the year. After a brief mid-season break which coincides in most years with the GCE examinations in June, the main part of the season begins, its first culmination being the National Long Course Championships, held in a 50-metre pool. The English Long Course Championships are open to swimmers from all over the world, but the Scottish and Welsh Long Course Championships were, until 1978 at least, open only to swimmers with certain qualifications of birth, residence, or parentage.

In most years the English Long Course Championships act as British trials for the major international games—the Olympic Games (held every fourth year, 1976, 1980, etc.), the World Championships (held in even years between Olympic years—1978, 1982, etc.), the European Championships (to be held every two years from 1981), and the Commonwealth Games (in even years between Olympic years). In addition there are international dual meet matches (e.g. Great Britain v. East Germany) and other team competitions, as well as an increasing number of minor international championship meets of an 'open meet' character.

Running parallel with the tree-like structure of the various national ASAs are the schools associations, and it is in these competitions that many talented swimmers who do not belong to swimming clubs are discovered.

From this you will have gathered that the structure of swimming roughly resembles a pyramid, with the clubs forming the base, the international teams the apex, with the swimmer having to negotiate the various strata of County, District and National competition on the way up. The same basic idea is present in every national organization however it is organized in detail. Some others, with more competitors than there are in Britain, have to grade their competitions

Swimmers and officials wait for the start at a Southern Counties meeting at London's Crystal Palace. District events are at an intermediate level in England, coming between the County and National competitions.

more carefully to see that all standards of ability are catered for.

The County, District and National competitions come round just once a year, and a swimmer would have a thin time if he could compete only in these. But enterprising clubs have instituted their own 'Open Meets' at which high-class competitors meet. Examples are the Southend and Leigh Multi-Nation meet and the Walthamstow meet, both of which have entries of near-national standard, but there are others on a lower level which, with the normal programme of inter-club competitions, should enable any swimmer of reasonable ability to gain improving competition.

The standard age-groups, in which swimmers compete against others of their own age and do not have to match themselves against those of more years are: 11 and under (the age being the birthday reached during the year of the competition), 12 and 13 years, 14 and 15 years, 16 and 17 years. There are variations on this framework, and other organizations may go down to 10 or 9 and under, or include 18-year-olds in the top band, but the idea is the same: to encourage swimmers to compete against their contemporaries and to allow them to develop at their own rate, not to expose them too soon against adult competitors. Of course, many swimmers reach international standard while they are only 14 or 15 years old and still compete as age-groupers. They have, though chosen to compete in the open age category events, whereas a few years ago, before the introduction of age-group swimming, they would have been restricted to senior (i.e. open) or junior events only.

A Summary of Swimming History

Outstanding swimming ability has been admired for centuries in all parts of the world. Until very late in the nineteenth century, though, swimmers who could swim for long distances were more admired than those who could swim fast. Swimming races held in Japan as early as 36 BC, and in AD 1603, by an Imperial edict, swimming became a part of the school curriculum. Swimming, or bathing at least, was popular among the Romans, but in Europe declining standards of hygiene resulted in a similar decline in the popularity of swimming. But watermanship was not universally neglected, as early in the nineteenth century the poet Lord Byron undertook several long swims for pleasure, one of which was a crossing of the Hellespont (between Europe and Asia, in Turkey) in honour and imitation of the Greek hero Leander.

Even so, we have to wait until February 1846 to find the first reference to a swimming 'championship'—a quarter-mile race won by a man called W. Redmond in Sydney, Australia. At this period there was almost an epidemic of sporting organization, especially in England

The widespread popularity of swimming is due partly to the exposure the sport has had on television. Here the annual Six Nations meet is transmitted on the Eurovision network.

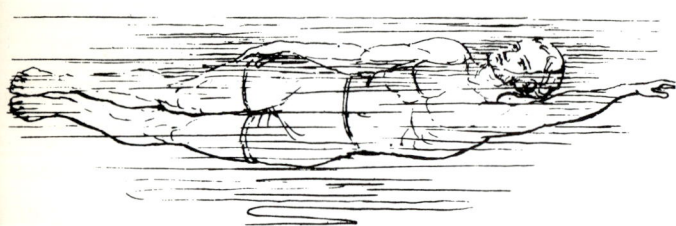

Fig 9

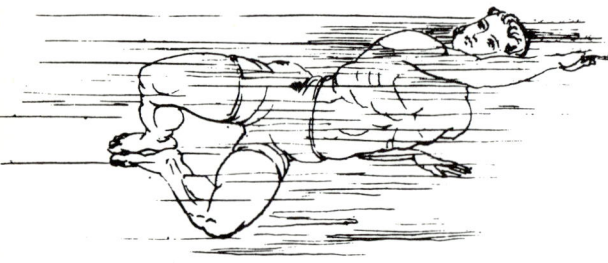

Fig 10

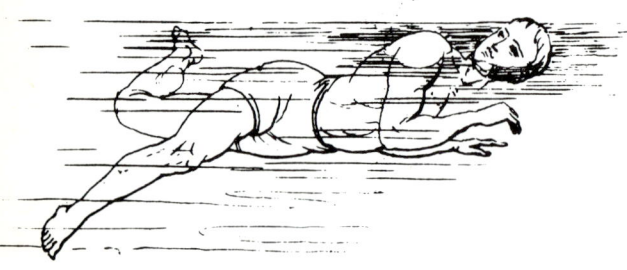

Fig 11

Steedman's sidestroke. 'In the attainment of speed it is unequalled', he wrote in the same year as Trudgen demonstrated his revolutionary double over-arm stroke.

where, in 1837, a National Swimming Association was formed. This body seems to have faded away but in 1869 the Metropolitan Swimming Clubs Association was formed in London, and this body in time developed into the present English Amateur Swimming Association.

The MSCA organized regular championships, beginning with a mile race in 1869, and by 1896 competitive swimming was popular enough to be included in the revived Olympic Games in Athens. Swimming has been a prominent feature of all subsequent Olympic Games. The world organizing body of swimming, the Fédération Internationale de Natation Amateur (FINA) was founded in 1908 during the Olympic Games being held in London, and since that date swimming has expanded in popularity to become a world sport with millions of participants.

Ever since modern competitive swimming started in the 1860s and 1870s there has been a continuous improvement in standards, so much so that many of today's age-group swimmers can produce times that not so many years ago would have been incredible even for a champion. Techniques too have been adjusted and improved beyond all recognition. Sadly the history of swimming technique is a neglected study, though perhaps it is understandable in a sport which is youth-orientated and forward looking rather than one always harking back to some forgotten golden age.

The first modern swimming style understandably resembled breaststroke, as it is the easiest stroke to swim slowly and the most useful in lifesaving. It was using breaststroke that Captain Webb swam across the English Channel in 1875.

When swum on the side with a 'screw' or asymmetrical leg kick the breaststroke became the side stroke, a faster technique than breaststroke. In sidestroke, one arm can recover (come forward to recommence the pulling action) above the water, making the stroke even faster. This single overarm stroke was used by many champions at the turn of the century, notably the Englishman John Arthur Jarvis and the German Emil Rausch, the last man to win a major freestyle title using sidestroke, at the St Louis Olympics of 1904.

Developing independently of the sidestroke was the Trudgen named after John Trudgen who first demonstrated the effectiveness of a double overarm stroke in winning a 160-yard handicap at Lambeth Baths in 1873. He used a form of breaststroke kick to each arm cycle. But opinion was that the Trudgen was only for sprinting.

Meanwhile in Australia a definite crawl stroke was emerging in which the legs kicked very little and the arms provided most of the propulsion. This crawl stroke spread to America and soon superseded the other strokes used in freestyle races, although Trudgen-like strokes were winning Olympic medals in the distance events as late as the 1920s.

From that time on the crawl stroke in one form

or another has dominated world freestyle swimming. There is still argument about the efficacy of the kick but there is a general consensus that different swimmers are adapted to different variations within the broad outline of the stroke.

Breaststroke has been preserved as a racing style only by the efforts of the lawyers and so has escaped the oblivion suffered by the sidestroke and Trudgen. An English 200 yards breaststroke championship was first held in 1903, and an Olympic 440 yards in 1904. A challenge to the classic style came in 1935 when some American swimmers experimented with a loophole in the laws and brought their arms forward over the water—the first butterfly strokes. This was then entirely within the rules, and for the following 20 years breaststroke races were split between the 'butterfly' and orthodox breaststrokers, and many swimmers used both styles in the same race. In 1952 official action by FINA split the butterfly away from breaststroke and a new stroke was recognized while an old loved one was preserved.

But once again a loophole in the breaststroke rules was exploited by ambitious swimmers who found they could swim the legal breaststroke faster underwater than on the surface, so spectators watched races in which the swimmers were only occasionally visible. Once more the rules were changed, in 1956, and since then the surface breaststroke has remained basically unaltered.

The butterfly, despite its breaststroke ancestry, has little in common with breaststroke today. The rules from the beginning did not specify a breaststroke kick, and the vertical reaction resulting from the arm action led to the adoption of the 'dolphin' kick. Butterfly swimmers using the breaststroke kick were soon outswum by the swifter and more graceful dolphin kickers, and the breaststroke–butterfly is now seldom seen at any more than the most elementary level.

Compared with the other strokes backstroke has had an uneventful history, with two main developments since it was first accorded the recognition of an English championship in 1903. Originally backstroke swimmers used a form of upside-down breaststroke, the so-called old-English backstroke. But the success of the front crawl pointed the way to a back crawl stroke, and it is this technique which has had no rivals in dorsal swimming since the first decade of this century. At first a limp arm recovery was fashionable, in imitation of the front crawl, but in the 1930s the American Adolph Keifer demonstrated the effectiveness of a straight arm recovery and pull. People were still striving after

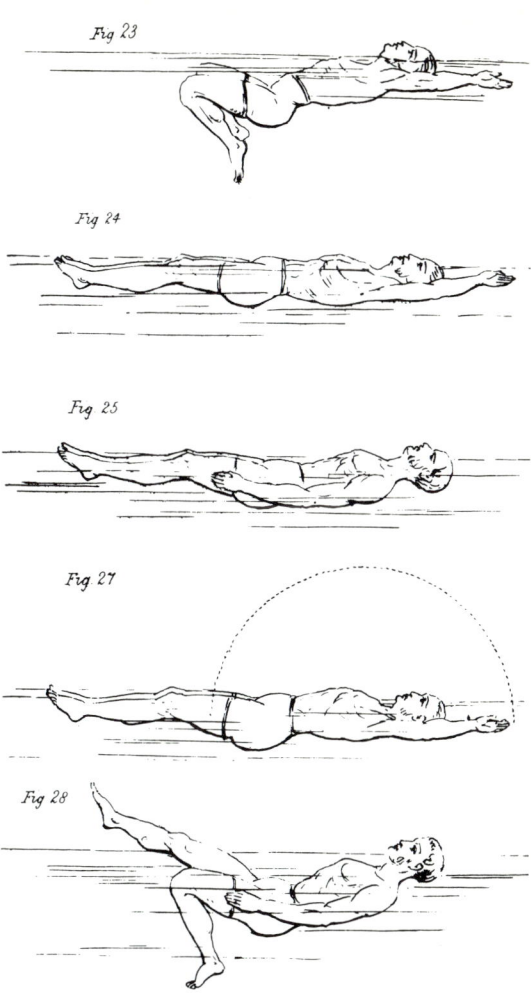

Techniques of swimming on the back, from Charles Steedman's Manual of Swimming (1873).

his oar-like arm pull in 1956 when an Australian, David Theile, adapted the bent arm pull—the 'S-pull'—and with it won the Olympic title. Theile's basic technique has been the model for successful backstrokers ever since.

Medley swimming came into the American programme in the 1920s but had to wait a long

Opposite above Commonwealth Games gold medallist Graeme Brewer is the latest in a line of Australian freestyle swimmers who can trace their ancestry to the earliest days of competitive swimming.

Opposite below Swimming champions come and go, but the East German backstroker Roland Matthes stayed at the top unbeaten in any backstroke race from 1967 to 1974.

time for world recognition. Relays were admitted to the Olympic Games in 1960 and an Individual Medley event in 1964. Only one year previously had there been an English IM championship!

Important Dates in Modern Swimming History

- 1869 Metropolitan Swimming Clubs Association, later the (English) Amateur Swimming Association, formed in London
First English championship held (men's 1 mile)
- 1873 John Trudgen swims 'Trudgen' stroke in London
- 1875 Captain Webb swims English Channel
- 1888 First Scottish championships (men's 100 and 220 yards)
- 1891 First Scottish ladies championship (200 yards)
- 1896 Modern Olympic Games established in Athens included swimming events
- 1900 First Olympic water polo tournament
- 1901 First English ladies championship (100 yards)
- 1904 Diving events introduced into Olympic programme
- 1908 Formation of Fédération Internationale de Natation Amateur (FINA)
Charles Daniels wins Olympic 100 metres title, so demonstrating superiority of crawl over Trudgen
- 1912 Ladies swimming and diving events added to Olympic programme
- 1924 Individual medley championships instituted in USA
Johnny Weissmuller (USA) wins three Olympic gold medals (100, 400, 4 x 200 metres freestyle)
- 1926 European swimming championships instituted
- 1930 British Empire (later Commonwealth) Games established
- 1935 'Butterfly' stroke first demonstrated in USA
- 1952 FINA separates butterfly and breaststroke, recognized world records for individual medley
- 1956 FINA bans underwater breaststroke and restricts world record list to long course times
- 1960 Medley relay events added to Olympic programme
- 1964 Individual medley events added to Olympic programme
Dawn Fraser (Australian) wins third successive Olympic title (100 metres freestyle)
- 1972 Electronic timing/place judging devices first used in Olympic Games in Munich during which Mark Spitz (USA) wins record seven gold medals
- 1973 World swimming championships, including swimming, diving, water polo, and synchronized swimming inaugurated

Appendix 1: Glossary

Some words and terms used in this book and in swimming generally with which you may not be familiar.

Age-group swimming A method of organizing swimming so that swimmers compete against others of their own age.

American crawl A now obsolete description of the front crawl with six leg beats to one arm cycle. So called as it was first popularized in the USA.

Australian crawl A front crawl stroke with two leg beats to one arm cycle was first swum in Australia, and hence this name. Australian freestylers still often swim with a modern version of this stroke.

Broken swim A training technique in which a swim of any distance is broken into shorter sections. The idea is to swim the race distance at faster than race speed.

Consolation final In some competitions the fastest swimmers who do not qualify for the final may swim in a consolation final, in an 8-lane pool for places 9 to 16.

Cross-over kick In front crawl some swimmers' legs will naturally kick on top of each other as the body rolls. It is nothing to be alarmed at if you have one.

Dolphin kick The double leg and body action of the butterfly kick.

False start A competitor starting before the signal commits a false start. There are recalls after the first two false starts but the perpetrator of a third, whether previously guilty or not, is automatically disqualified.

Fast pool A pool in which fast times may be expected, normally because of the design of the pool itself.

Final The fastest swimmers in the heats qualify for the final, being assigned lanes according to the spearhead principle.

First stroke A swimmer's first stroke may be defined as the stroke with which he most closely approaches the world's best. A swimmer's first stroke often changes year by year as he improves in different areas.

Flags These are strung across the pool, usually 5 metres out, to warn the backstrokers of the imminence of the turn.

Goggles Used to protect the eyes and are now almost universal among swimmers in training and races. Be sure yours don't come off and hamper you during a race. Follow the safety instructions.

Heats Preliminary rounds in an event. Swimmers may be distributed in one of three ways: at random; by seeding, whereby the faster swimmers are systematically distributed throughout the draw; by grading, in which the swimmers are arranged in time order, the fastest swimmers having the high numbers. Progression from heats to finals is on time alone.

Individual medley An individual race broken into four equal sections of butterfly, backstroke, breaststroke and freestyle (a different stroke to the others, usually front crawl).

Judges In swimming competitions there are three kinds of judge. Stroke judges check that all swimmers conform to the rules of the stroke; turn judges rule on the legality of a swimmer's turns; placing judges adjudicate on the order of finishing and act as turning judges at the finishing end. Note: a judge's decision is final and may not be overruled, however wrong you might think he is.

Junior Under 17 in the year of competition or, for junior record purposes, under 17 on the day of the swim.

Kick Part of the stroke performed by the legs.

Kicking Training drill using the legs only.

Kicking board Buoyant board of cork or plastic used to support body in kicking practices.

Lane Part of pool divided from the rest by rope divider.

Life saving Swimming activity in which skills of rescuing people in difficulties in the water is practised, together with resuscitation techniques.

Long course 50-metre or (rarely) 55-yard pool.

Main stroke The stroke which the swimmer considers his or her best. Usually, but not always, the first stroke.

Masters swimming Age-group swimming for older swimmers. The age bands normally cover five or ten years and start at 25 years old.

Medley relay A relay race for four swimmers covering equal legs of (in this order) backstroke, breaststroke, butterfly, and freestyle (i.e. front crawl). See **Individual medley**.

Negative split To swim the second half of a distance race faster than the first.

Open turn A turn during which the head stays out of the water, as it does in breaststroke and butterfly turns and in some freestyle turns.

Paddles Training aids attached to the hands for strengthening and technical practices.

Personal survival Skill of saving one's own life in the water, including floating using clothing, underwater swimming, swimming while clothed, etc.

Plunging Diving for distance, once a popular competitive event but now rarely seen.

Pull Part of the stroke performed by the arms.

Pull buoy Buoyant device for supporting legs during pulling practice.

Pulling Training drill using the arms only.

Record World records are recognized by FINA for the following individual events for men and women: freestyle 100, 200, 400, 800, 1500 metres; breaststroke 100, 200 metres; butterfly 100, 200 metres; backstroke 100, 200 metres; individual medley 200, 400 metres; relays, men: 4 x 100 medley, 4 x 100 and 4 x 200 freestyle; relays, women: 4 x 100 medley, 4 x 100 freestyle. National, District, and County records follow this pattern with some variations, often with two sets of records for long and short course swimming.

Recovery Part of the stroke during which the limb (arm or leg) is moving back to the start of its propulsive movement, for example the over the water action of the arms in the crawl strokes.

Referee Official in charge of a swimming competition and responsible for its smooth running and for deciding in cases where the judges are not in agreement.

Relays Team races in swimming come in two

Lightweight goggles have been a blessing to swimmers who might formerly have been resigned to living with sore eyes: make sure yours fit and stay on!

main forms: medley (see **Medley relay**) and freestyle (in which any stroke may be swum, though almost always front crawl). Swimmers take over from each other at the end of the pool, and the incoming swimmer must have touched the end before the outgoing swimmer's feet leave the block.

Schedule List of training to be done in a session.

Session A period spent training.

Short course Pools less than 50 metres long, but held to refer to only 25-yard or 25-metre courses by some purists.

Slow pool A pool in which waves build up and in which fast times are not to be expected.

Spearhead The arrangement of swimmers in a final or seeded heat whereby, in an eight-lane pool, the fastest swimmer or qualifier is placed in lane 4, the second fastest in lane 5, and so on in lanes 3, 6, 2, 7, and 1 until the slowest swimmer is in lane 8.

Split An intermediate time during a race.

Squad A group of swimmers joined together for training, either within a club or from a combination of clubs.

Start The beginning of a race. In backstroke the swimmers start in the water. In the other strokes a dive start is made. Once the swimmers are standing on the back of their blocks the starter's command is 'Take your marks!'. They immediately take up their starting position on the front of the block and when they are perfectly still the starter will give the starting signal.

Starter Official responsible for the start of a race.

Starting-block Raised platform from which swimmer starts race, incorporating grips for backstrokers starting in the water.

Timed final In some longer events only heats are held, with no final, the result being declared from heat times only. Such races should be graded, with the fastest swimmers going together in the final heat. Sometimes known as the declared winner system.

Timekeeper Official responsible for taking a swimmer's time.

Touch Act of finishing length prior to turn or at the finish.

Warm up Brief period of acclimatization to exercise and, if possible, competition pool before a race. Properly warmed-up swimmers swim better than those not warmed up.

Appendix 2: Laws of Swimming

The full laws of swimming cover many pages, but the following are especially relevant to the swimmer himself and to swimming competition. Full copies of the laws as applied in England may be obtained from the Amateur Swimming Association, Harold Fern House, Derby Square, Loughborough, Leicestershire LE11 0AL.

115. Officials
i. A decision upon a question of fact by the appropriate official shall be final.

118. Starting (except Backstroke; see 124.)
A.
i. The starter shall take up a position at the side of the course. The competitors, on a signal from the starter (or referee) shall step on to the rear of the starting blocks or stand a short pace back from the edge of the starting line, or enter the water as required by Laws 121–124.
ii. on the preparatory command from the starter 'Take your marks', the competitors shall immediately take up a starting position either on the front of the starting block or line ... and shall remain stationary until the starter gives the starting signal.
B. In the event of a false start:
i. ... the starter shall call back the competitors at the first or second false start. After two false starts the starter shall warn the competitors that the race will proceed at the third attempt irrespective of further infringement. The starter shall disqualify any offending competitor at the third start whether he was a previous offender or not.
ii. ... a rope shall be used for the purpose of stopping competitors in the even of a false start. Wherever possible the false start rope shall be suspended across the pool from fixed stands placed 15 metres in front of the starting end, attached to the stands by a quick release mechanism.

119. Team races
The team of a competitor whose feet, or hands in the case of a swimmer starting in the water, have lost touch with his starting place before his preceding partner touches the end shall be disqualified, unless the competitor in default returns to his starting place at the wall. It shall not be necessary to remount the starting platform.

120. The race
(b) Standing. A competitor does not disqualify himself in a freestyle race by standing upon the bottom of the bath or course for the purpose of resting, but he shall not walk.

121. Freestyle swimming
A competitor may start with a plunge or jump, or in the water holding the rail or side of the bath or other starting place. A competitor may swim any style or styles and rules relating to breast, butterfly and backstroke swimming shall not apply. In freestyle turning and finishing the swimmer may touch the wall with any part of his body. A hand touch is not obligatory.

122. Breaststroke swimming
(a) A competitor may start with a plunge or jump, or in the water, facing the course, and holding the rail, or side of the bath or other starting place, with both hands.
(b) The body shall be kept perfectly on the breast and both shoulders shall be in line with the water surface from the beginning of the first arm stroke after the start and after the turn.
(c) All movements of the legs and arms shall be simultaneous and in the same horizontal plane without alternating movement.
(d) The hands shall be pushed forward together from the breast and shall be brought back on or under the surface of the water.
(e) In the leg kick the feet shall be turned outwards in the backward movement. A 'dolphin' kick is not permitted.
(f) At the turn, and upon finishing the race, the touch shall be made with both hands, simultaneously at the same level either at, above, or below the water level and with the shoulders in the horizontal position.

The grab start is the most reliable and quickest method of getting off the starting block. Multi-Olympic medallist Shirley Babashoff (block No. 4) shows how it's done.

(g) A part of the head shall always be above the general water level, except that at the start and at each turn the swimmer may take one arm stroke and one leg kick while wholly submerged.

123. Butterfly stroke

(a) A competitor may start with a plunge or jump, or in the water, facing the course, and holding the rail, or side of the bath or other starting place, with both hands.

(b) Both arms shall be brought forward over the water and brought backward simultaneously.

(c) The body shall be kept perfectly on the breast and both shoulders in line with the surface of the water from the beginning of the first arm stroke, after the start and after the turn.

(d) All movements of the feet shall be executed in a simultaneous manner. Simultaneous up and down movements of the legs and feet in the vertical plane are permitted. The legs or feet need not be at the same level but no alternating movement is permitted.

(e) When touching at the turn or on finishing a race, the touch shall be made with both hands simultaneously on the same level, and with the shoulders in the horizontal position. The touch may be made at, above, or below the water level.

(f) At the start and at turns, a swimmer is permitted one or more leg kicks and one arm pull under the water, which shall bring him to the surface.

124. Backstroke swimming

(a) Competitors shall line up in the water facing the starting end with hands on the end, rail, or starting grips. The feet, including the toes, shall be under the surface of the water. Standing in or on the gutter or bending the toes over the lip of the gutter is prohibited.

(b) At the signal for starting and after the turn they shall push off and swim upon their backs throughout the race. The hands shall not be released before the starting signal has been given.

(c) Any competitor leaving his normal position on the back before the head, foremost hand, or arm has touched the end of the course for the purpose of turning or finishing shall be disqualified.

(d) Wherever possible backstroke turn indicators shall be provided by means of flagged ropes suspended across the pool 1.8 metres above the water surface from fixed supports or stands set 5 metres from each end wall of the pool. Clarification of turn. It is permissible to turn over beyond the vertical after the foremost part of the body has touched, for the purpose of executing the turn, but the swimmer shall have returned past the vertical to a position on his back before the feet have left the wall.

125. Medley swimming

Medley events shall consist of equal legs or four strokes in the following order:

(a) Individual medley—Butterfly, Backstroke, Breaststroke, Freestyle.

(b) Medley relay—Backstroke, Breaststroke, Butterfly, Freestyle.

In medley events, Freestyle shall be any stroke other than Butterfly, Backstroke, or Breaststroke.

Useful Addresses

ASSOCIATIONS

Amateur Swimming Association (England)
Secretary N. W. Sarsfield, MC,
Harold Fern House,
Derby Square,
Loughborough,
Leics LE11 0AL

Scottish ASA
Hon. Secretary W. Black,
Pathfoot Building,
University of Stirling,
Stirling FK9 4LA

Welsh ASA
Hon. Secretary J. A. Jones-Pritchard,
21 Old Vicarage Close,
Llanifhen,
Cardiff

Irish ASA
Hon. Secretary N. A. Green,
6 Maywood Crescent,
Dublin 5

British Long Distance Swimming Association
Hon. General Secretary J. K. Slater,
45 Farnley Lane,
Otley,
West Yorkshire

Swimming Teachers Association
1 Birmingham Road,
West Bromwich,
West Midlands
B71 4JQ

British Swimming Coaches Association
General Secretary H. E. Bland,
Dormer House,
13 Dormer Place,
Leamington Spa,
Warwickshire CV32 5AA

Amateur Swimming Union of Australia
PO Box 1504,
North Sydney,
NSW 2060

Aquatic Federation of Canada
333 River Road,
Ottawa K1L 8B9

New Zealand ASA
PO Box 22–723,
High Street,
Christchurch

Amateur Athletic Union of the United States
AAU House
3400 West 86th Street,
Indianapolis,
Indiana 46268

MAGAZINES

Swimming Times (Great Britain)
Harold Fern House,
Derby Square,
Loughborough,
Leicestershire LE11 0AL

Swimming World (USA)
8622 Bellanca Avenue,
Los Angeles,
California 90045

Swim (Canada)
402 King Street East,
Toronto,
Ontario M5A 1L3

Ron McKeon of Australia, gold medallist 200 m and 400 m freestyle, Commonwealth Games, Edmonton 1978.

Chris Jarvis (England) leads Jane Lowe (NZ) in 100 m breaststroke, Commonwealth Games, Christchurch 1974.

Sharron Davies, Britain's double gold medallist, 1978.

Hungary's Zoltan Verrazto.

Wendy Cook, Canada's world record holder in 100 m backstroke.